BUILDING A STATE OF RESPONSIBLE DEMOCRACY

About the Author

Algimantas Valentinas Indriūnas is an engineer, a doctor of social sciences and a journalist. He is also an active figure in the social and political life of Lithuania.

In 1941, he and his family were exiled by the Soviet government to Altai Krai, and a year later, in 1942 to Yakutia (Sakha Republic) on the shores of the Laptev sea (in the far North of Asia). There he graduated from a local high school, and started working as a projectionist (cinema projector operator). These areas of GULAG (Soviet forced labor camp system) were dense with prisoners, which sparked his interest in understanding their world views, values, aspirations, etc. He applied the accumulated knowledge in some of his works.

In late 1946, he escaped from exile and returned to Lithuania with falsified documents and had a successful career until the regaining of Lithuania's independence, He was initially employed as a projectionist in Kaunas, and enrolled in the Kaunas Polytechnic Institute (currently Kaunas University of Technology), from where he graduated with a major in cinema mechanics. He served as the principal of the school of cinema mechanics (currently Kaunas Information Technology School) until 1959, when he became assistant editor of the popular Lithuanian journal "Science and Technology" where he later served as the chief editor until 1973, when revelations about of some of the facts of the exile of his family led to his removal from office.

In 1975, he started work as a lecturer, head of department, dean of the faculty, and associate professor in the People's Economic Development Institute (later named the Lithuanian Academy of Management).

He defended his dissertation in Lomonosov Moscow State University, and was awarded doctorate in the field of management of social systems.

In 2000-2004, he was elected a member of the Lithuanian parliament, and in 2004 he received a national award for his contributions to Lithuania.

Research interests: management and governance.

THIS PAGE IS INTENTIONALLY LEFT BLANK

BUILDING A STATE OF RESPONSIBLE DEMOCRACY

ALGIMANTAS VALENTINAS INDRIŪNAS

2016
Vilnius

Publisher: Algimantas Valentinas Indriūnas
Country: Republic of Lithuania

E-mail: a.v.indriunas@gmail.com
Mailing list: responsible-democracy@googlegroups.com

Acknowledgements: The invaluable advice and assistance given by Name(s) and / or Company Name and Name(s) and / or Company Name is acknowledged by the Publisher. Thanks are also due to Name(s) and / or Company Name and members of the Company Name User Group for their advice. The Author(s) wish(es) to acknowledge the help of Name, Name, and Name in developing this book. Name(s) acknowledges the support of their / his / her family(ies). Name(s) acknowledges the support of Name(s) and Name(s). The Publisher also acknowledges the input of Name(s) who have / has worked through the book meticulously.

Title: Building A State of Responsible Democracy

Translated by: Evelina Čapkevičiūtė © 2016
Edited by: Siobhán Denham © 2016
Page Design: documentfoundation.org

ISBN: 978-609-408-735-6

Printed and Bound: Lulu.com.

Contents

INTRODUCTION

The ideal of democracy in the political life of modern society is one of the most valuable political ideals. However, it is also the one that causes the most debate among the brightest minds. Seeing it as an aspiration to inspire mankind to deal with the problems of social conflict and political justice, we must get to the root of what democracy means in our lives, the ways it is expressed and the problems we face when we try to implement it. The brightest minds have posed both the pros and the cons of democracy, having studied the period of its evolution that spans more than two thousand years.[1] Leaving aside the philosophical debate, we will try to explain the current flaws of democracy and look for practical and easily attainable ways of dealing with them so that democracy could ensure happier lives for the people of any country.

It is hard to imagine a modern democratic state without a universally accepted constitution (i.e. by means of national referendum) through which citizens retain certain rights, while at the same time granting specific authorities to the government that it is not allowed to exceed. Recently there have been allegations that too many constitutional regulations legitimizing all sorts of restrictions (immunities) are being proposed, which may be restrictive to democracy while also limiting the sovereignty of the nation. We are of the opinion that democracy remains intact, provided that, aside from the minimally required rules of "one vote per person" and the simple principle of the rule of majority, other provisions are enforced, such as ensuring the safety of people, justice, formal equality, the positive

---

1 D. Held, Models of Democracy. (see chapters 9 and 10).

freedom of an individual, supervising the division of power and governmental competence.[2]

Those who wish to defend the interests of the richest people in the world (those who make up 1 percent of the world's population and own 48 percent of the world's capital, according to the data of 2014), the so-called "Chicago boys" along with them, blame democracy calling it "the tyranny of the majority" and suggest adopting supermajority rule or weighted voting, cumulative voting, mixed constitutions, executive discretion, judicially protected rights, quadratic voting models and methods instead, which may be more or less suitable for privately owned companies and for making various working group decisions, but not for the processes of a democratically ruled state, because they violate the basic "one vote" and "majority rule" principles and do not provide any protection against dead-ends or the risks of corruption.

Aspiring to create the most rational model of democracy that it is possible to attain, we will subscribe to the scientific point of view. In science, every law, rule, provision, method, experiment or any other result of a scientific investigation – no matter how renowned it may be in the scientific world – is allowed to be repeated, verified, criticized, denied or suggested to be replaced by a new one. If any one of these actions were to be limited by any means, denied or allowed to remain the status quo, the process would cease to be science and become dogma, which is often connected to something that doesn't exist and cannot exist or something that is doubted.

Any process of creation, given that one wants to develop something essentially new, involves the denial of something old, or dated. As an old French saying goes, "you can't make an omelet without breaking eggs", which is why we shouldn't be surprised that in order to create the most rational democratic model in

---

2 J.E. Lane, Constitutions and Political Theory. (see chapter 11. Democracy and constitutionality).

our opinion, we will have to analyze, criticize or even deny some truths of state administration that have been well-established and universally accepted, as well as various provisions such as resolutions of the United Nations, The Universal Declaration of Human Rights, or materials by the European Union and other cross-border arrangement documents. That doesn't mean that all of them or at least some of them will have to be rejected. At this point we are only considering such a possibility.

In this book we will discuss the necessity of governmental reform, the most common flaws of democracy, the means and measures that need to be taken in order to avoid them or at least to minimize their destructive influence, the reform of political parties as one of the main institutions of the political life of the state, the advantages of a two-house parliamentary system, the dangers of presidential rule, the reform of municipal government, the harm brought by corruption and the death penalty issue.

The author doesn't think of himself to be an indisputable authority when it comes to questions of state governance or to consider the implementation of the propositions and recommendations suggested in this book to be compulsory and immediate in the governmental system of a given state. The aim of the book is to provoke a discussion about the issues presented in it. We get the worst results when society accepts the problems and doesn't make any effort to alleviate the situation. However, when people reflect on the problems and start talking about them, begin discussions or start looking for answers, a better solution or at least a satisfactory one is normally found and life becomes better. That is precisely what the author of the book wishes for his readers.

1

Characteristics of Some of the Concepts

In order to avoid a useless dispute, let's consider some of the characteristics of language. To start off, language is a polymorphic thing. In most cases one term or one word can have several meanings. For example, while analyzing the concept of culture, Abraham A. Moles notes that the word "culture" has more than 250 definitions.[3] Or, as another example, an architect, a shoemaker, a clothes designer or a mathematician will ascribe completely different meanings to the word "model", having heard it out of context. These meanings will be fundamentally different from one another and from the definition we use when we say "model".

A party, according to the dictionary of international terms, is: 1) a political organization of like-minded individuals that has a certain authority or aims to have one; 2) a group of individuals established in order to perform a certain task; 3) a certain amount of items, most of the time sent or received; 4) one complete game, from start to finish;

3 A.A. Moles, Sociodynamique de la culture.

5) a component of a musical composition; 6) a spouse. A party in the first sense is usually called a political party, but for the sake of simplicity in this book we will refer only to a political party when we use the stand-alone term. The term "party" itself comes from the Latin "pars, partis" and implies that it is a part of something, in our case – a part of the society of a certain state, or – to put it simply – a part of a nation. The analysis of the evolution of parties shows that they are usually formed by a certain separate class of society which is brought together by a common political interest. The organization that is thus formed is usually identical to a party; however, sometimes it can be called a front, a movement, a union, an association, a league, or referred to by some other name. It must be noted that a party might also be established under a different pretext than the one stated here.

Politics. The first person to define this term was Aristotle, who dedicated one of his larger works to political analysis.[4] According to Aristotle, politics is the art of ruling a state. It must be noted that the philosophers of Ancient Greece, Aristotle and Plato among them, usually use the term "art" when they refer to a technology as a process. That is why in their understanding a carpenter's art or a cobbler's art is a valid thing. Today we call this process a technology. That is why when we stumble upon the word "politics" in this book, we must understand that the discussion is about the technology of governing a state. It can be both good and bad, it persists and will continue existing in any way a state is governed. If there is a state, it is implied that a certain governing process also exists, and along with it – the technology of governing the state, which is what we call politics. In the author's opinion, it would be incorrect for an educated person to speak about the end of politics as it is spoken in many works by Carl Marx and his followers, and likewise in Francis Fukuyama's The End of

4 Aristotle in Twenty-three Volumes. Vol. 21. Politics.

History, according to which humans will begin leading a dog's life as humanity continues its existence.

Political science. If we think of politics as a technology used for the administration of government matters, then political science could be seen as the science behind this technology. Political scientists, in our opinion, can look at facts about past events objectively, interpret them in their own way, but they cannot present them one-sidedly, or present only the ones they do agree with and ignore the rest, they cannot distort them. This would make them political forgers rather than political scientists. But political scientists do have the right to assess and criticize the actions of the government and the current system, make forecasts about the future or suggest hypotheses and solutions based on objective facts about past events.

A state is a sovereign society of people in a certain defined territory, governed by the local official institutions. It is said that the state was built and nurtured through the human need for safety. It is true that for the past few hundred years Westerners, as well as some of those of other countries have been provided with a safe and civilized life with the help of a sovereign state.

Government – the political system by which a nation or community is administrated and regulated.

To govern – to control and manage an area, city or country and its people.

Management – the control and operation of a business organization. Usually the term "management" refers to business, in which one of the most important things (although maybe not the most important one) in our opinion is profit, when in the case of the term "to govern" the main things are the quality of the services and their smallest price. Trying to reach profitability in the case of governing might involve a negative effect, meaning an increase in the price of services.

Self-governance refers to the right and ability of locally elected officials to administer and govern part of the public interest responsibly and in the interests of the local people. This right is exercised by a confidential, equal, immediate and general vote by an elected council of representatives that can have its own executives. Aside from that, any other form of citizen participation in the governance of state such as citizens' assemblies, referendums or opinion polls can operate at the self-governance level.

Mission, purpose – [1. an object to be attained; a thing intended; 2. the intention to act;] – this is usually the policy and aim of a group of people, an organization, although it can sometimes be that of an individual as well. In speaking terms, it is usually called a goal. But goals always have to be defined in time not only qualitatively but also in a quantifiable form, in order to see if the they have been reached at a certain point, whereas a mission is a type of goal which can be quite undefined and constantly reached for, such as "making people's lives better", "decreasing the number of traffic accidents", etc. It is the limit one wants to reach but can always only approach closer and closer.

An objective – something that you are trying to achieve. In our opinion, this is the desired result of some activity or movement which is planned to be reached in a certain time. If we wish to use an objective as an instrument for the administration of political life, we must insist that the objective be specific, defined in time during which it is hoped to be achieved and also expressed in such a form that when that time comes we would be able to check if this objective has been reached or not.

An aim – 1. a purpose or design; an object aimed at; 2. the directing of a weapon, missile, etc., at an object. II. 1. The purpose of doing sth; what sb. is trying to achieve; the action or skill of pointing a weapon at sb/sth.

A goal – the object of a person's ambition, effort; a destination; an aim. This coincides with the term used in football as well.

Political freedom – this book deals with the topic of political freedom. There can be two conceptions of freedom. A negative conception of freedom is the lack of intervention by others into the choices of an individual. A positive conception of freedom is that the individual is the master of his or her own affairs and can choose to do one thing and not the other, to be a certain way and not the other. According to I. Kant, political freedom is inseparable from the concept of political violence. The goal of politics is creating an order by which the needs of all individuals are combined through an equally obliging principle. In certain situations, the *laws of the* state can restrict the freedom of an individual in order to conserve the interests of society.

Constitution is the law of *laws that is the basis for the creation of all other laws, adopted through a general referendum. To put it simply, the* constitution differs from all other *laws by the fact that all other laws are issued by the government in* order for the people to follow them, when the constitution is the law adopted by the people for the government to abide. The people keep certain defined rights through the constitution and appoint powers to the government that it cannot trespass.

Democracy *(Greek, demos – the nation, cratos – government, altogether meaning the rule of the nation)* in the wider sense is the form of ruling a state where the power comes from the will of the people. Currently two main forms of democracy are distinguished:

- **Direct democracy** – a form of democracy where the citizens of the state vote on the most important national questions through assemblies or referendums and assign their execution to executive organizations.

Representative democracy – a form of democracy where the citizens elect officials through a general election and give them the power to administrate the state in their name.

Democracy has had a long and complicated path of evolution and transformation. If we inspect the processes of a sovereign state and representative democracy closer, we have to concede that as Pierre Manent has indicated, due to processes that began at the end of the last century, the state has started becoming less sovereign, and the rule – less representative.[5]

The principle of the correlation of duties, rights and responsibilities. Human rights are often talked about, but it is almost never mentioned that these rights can only be granted when people feel the duty to protect the rights of everyone else of protecting everyone else's rights and are able to feel the responsibility for it. If nobody were to feel responsible for the protection of everyone's person's rights, human rights would become an empty declaration. Which means that duty is worth more than a right, and the reason why so many bad things happen today is because everyone – even children – know their rights, but don''t know their duties or forget them. So, in order to create a responsible democracy, we must adhere to the principle of the correlation of duties, rights and responsibility. Putting this principle into effect means that every duty performed must entail certain rights granted along with it and no right can be granted that is not needed for the duty to be performed. Every right has to have a certain responsibility and no responsibility should be required for an act which was committed without a certain right involved.

In order for a person to be able to use the rights granted him by the state, governmental institutions and their officials, as well as others must have a duty to ensure the actualization of those rights. Proper responsibility for evasion of duty and indifference to the interests of people must be determined. A state of responsible democracy, which this

5 P. Manent, La raison des Nations. Reflections sur la democratie en Europe.

book is dedicated to, can only be created once the principle of the correlation of duties, rights and responsibility is fully brought into play.

2
The Relevance of State Reform

The matter of state government reform becomes relevant especially due to the fact that lately the political lives of some countries have not only been of exceptionally low-quality, but amoral as well, ruled by oligarchy and constantly fostering social exclusion. The poor are becoming poorer while the rich get richer. As social alienation and people's dissatisfaction with government grows, social tension increases as well. According to the theory of catastrophism, as social tension increases, at a certain critical point, it takes only a tiny impulse for the situation to get out of hand – which in turn starts a revolution. All revolutions tear down the existing order, but usually they fare far worse in creating a new one, and that's how turmoil starts and it is the common people that suffer the most, although there are those who acquire undeserved wealth during the process, as well as those who obtain power and foster totalitarianism.

We should not wait for a revolutionary situation to arise. Society must be concerned with making reforms when the time is right if the state is to remain a parliamentary republic, and for politics to become a practice that deserves respect, for politicians to keep in touch with their elective body and work in their interests. If we were to look for the reasons of why today's state governance has been so unsuccessful, we would find that it is because the majority of *laws grant certain* rights to institutions, but do not determine personal responsibilities for collegial decisions, which harm citizens and the state.

At the present time, it is hard to determine who has to answer for flawed reforms in most countries, the squander of national wealth and privatization funds, the growth of foreign credit and the irrational use of it, the deficit of current accounts, the extent of corruption, monopoly rights granted to investors, the rise of crime, the differentiation of property, bankruptcies of economic enterprises, the unfavorable situation for business growth and the creation of new jobs, the constantly deteriorating lives of many people. The fact that isolated cases of crime are punished does not solve the fundamental problems. Although the constitutions of some countries, such as France[6], Italy[7] and Spain[8] do intend to convict members of the state for crimes performed during years in office, most politicians successfully manage to avoid this criminal responsibility.

It is also very important to consider the constantly growing political indifference of people. It is a bad sign for the state. History shows that political indifference has been

---

6 **Constitution of France.** Title X - On the Criminal Liability of Members of the Government.

Article 68-1

- Members of the Government shall be criminally liable for acts performed in the holding of their office and classified as serious crimes or other major offences at the time they were committed.
- They shall be tried by the Court of Justice of the Republic.
- The Court of Justice of the Republic shall be bound by such definition of serious crimes and other major offences and such determination of penalties as are laid down by statute.

Article 68-2

- The Court of Justice of the Republic shall consist of fifteen members: twelve Members of Parliament, elected in equal number from among their ranks by the National Assembly and the Senate after each general or partial renewal by election of these Houses, and three judges of the Cour de cassation, one of whom shall preside over the Court of Justice of the Republic.
- Any person claiming to be a victim of a serious crime or other major offence committed by a member of the Government in the holding of his office may lodge a complaint with a petitions committee.
- This committee shall order the case to be either closed or forwarded to the Chief Public Prosecutor at the Cour de cassation for referral to the Court of Justice of the Republic.
- The Chief Public prosecutor at the Cour de cassation may also make a referral ex officio to the Court of Justice of the Republic with the assent of the petitions committee. An Institutional Act shall determine the manner in which this article is to be implemented.

Article 68-3

- The provisions of this title shall apply to acts committed before its entry into force.

7 **Constitution of Italy.**

Article 96.

- The President of the Council of Ministers and the Ministers, even if they resign from office, are subject to normal justice for crimes committed in the exercise of their duties, provided authorisation is given by the Senate of the Republic or the Chamber of Deputies, in accordance with the norms established by Constitutional Law.

8 **Constitution of Spain.**

Article 1021.

the ruin of many a state. When citizens are passive government control loosens and lawlessness thrives, *laws are ignored, corruption takes root, despotism rises and the conditions needed for dark forces to influence the government arise. The government loses its independence and weakens. The* state becomes susceptible to outside influence, it is invaded or annexed and disappears from the world map. That has happened to many countries – in the 5th century Rome was among them,[9] as well as the Polish-Lithuanian Commonwealth in the 18th century.

On the other hand, when citizens become politically active, determined to protect their own rights and freedoms at any cost, even a subdued country that has lost its independence can beat an invading state that is superior both in military and economic terms, and may once again take its rightful place among the other countries. The resolution and unity of the people often proves to be stronger than invading tanks. Such examples do exist. The economic and military power of Great Britain and France were much stronger than that of the resistance in their colonies – India and Algeria. However, they granted independence to their former colonies because of the integrity and peaceful protest of the people. It was becoming harder and harder to keep the colonies and it was no longer profitable.

A conscious citizen shouldn't remain indifferent and satisfy himself with simply stating the fact when he observes

1. The President and other members of the Government shall be held criminally liable, should the occasion arise, before the Criminal Section of the Supreme Court.
2. If the charge is of treason or of any offence against the security of the State committed in the exercise of their office, it may only be brought on the initiative of one quarter of the members of Congress and with the approval of the absolute majority thereof.
3. The Royal prerogative of pardon shall not be applicable in any of the cases provided for under the present article.

9 476 A.D., even though some of the sources doubt this date.

the political indifference of the majority of the people in any country. After all, it isn't only the people's fault that they are indifferent to politics. The conditions they are in are also to blame. We do not have the moral right to stand by passively while our nation is in danger. Every honest citizen must look for a solution to situations that put their nation and state in danger. If we are to do that we must find the causes for political indifference and suggest ways to remove them. We cannot claim that there are no progressive ideas.

If we wish to remain honest, we cannot close our eyes to wrongdoing, to people's failed expectations, to the big, as well as the small mistakes, that the government makes along with the provisional measures designed to prevent dangers as well. With these conditions in mind, we must ask ourselves if there really is nothing we can do to turn the lives of people around, and if there is - what is it and how should it be carried out? However, one thing is clear: as many difficulties of life that we list, as much as we complain against the government, as much as we condemn the parties, life does not and will not get better from making a list.

On the other hand, we must consider that only those who do nothing make no mistakes. To err is human, and this is true also for governments. We cannot live in a wrong way just because we cannot cheat the reality of life. An unseen or hidden error will always play a disruptive or harmful role. Our goal is not to condemn any particular government for its errors, but to find ways to avoid similar errors in the future, to find ways of solving relevant problems. That means that it is very important to correct mistakes in time and therefore the people who find, point out and stress the mistakes should not be feared because that is how the chance to fix them arises sooner.

Immediate action for the advancement of democracy should also be taken because recently it has been criticized much more often than before. A lot of the authors who denounce democracy tend to have overtones of nostalgia for totalitarianism. Democracy is being bad-mouthed in all kinds of ways, with claims that it supposedly came from a pathos of freedom, the recognition of integral human rights, conscience and freedom of speech. However, the meaningless understanding of freedom hides a darker side, which brings the destruction of spiritual freedom and an indifference to spirituality. Some authors refer to Plato when they claim that democracy is a manufactured evil and that too much freedom leads to disorder and opens the way for the rise of tyranny. We must admit that in the dawn on his work Plato has pointed out the flaws of democracy in The Republic, dubbing it the worst form of state government. But we must note that later on he revised his opinion and conceded in The Statesman[10] that given a state where *laws are not complied with,* democracy is the best form of state government because it is the least prone to allow trespass. That is why the unconditional bad-mouthing of democracy with reference to Plato should be deemed incorrect and unacceptable in a scientific society.

It is wonderful to observe that there are contrary opinions. It is claimed that when a state is ruled poorly, everybody knows it and nobody really doubts it, apart from some of the politicians. The word 'democracy' is not to blame here. What makes democracy seem disreputable is the fact that the wrong people have been elected to represent society. We can replace the word, but will it make things better? That's why the name should not be loathed and instead ways to improve democracy to what the previous generations hoped it would be should be offered instead.

10 Plato. Statesman. London: Routledge & Kegan Paul, 1952.

At the same time, nobody happens to complain about democracy in Switzerland – the oldest democratic state in the world. Maybe we should analyze the experience of a state that shows due respect to democracy in more depth.

Nothing – an item, a system or a method – is not and cannot be either completely good or completely bad. Any single thing we choose has both good sides as well as bad sides. A strategy of improvement first requires us to find out both the good and the bad sides, and then take action in order to remove the bad ones or at least minimize their influence. At the same time, every opportunity must be taken to improve the good sides as well. We shall try to use the same method in this work also, as it would be suitable for the improvement of democracy in any state and at the same time for the improvement of the administrative processes in it. This means that the first step we shall take will be to find the *flaws of* democracy or other issues that arise in the process of state government, and then we shall look for ways to remove them or minimize their influence on the quality of people's lives, so that we can take action in order to improve democracy, as well as the processes of state government, so that not only would it work as efficiently, but even better than it does in some of the leading countries of the world.

We cannot expect parliament members to handicap themselves and surrender their privileges. However, the unity of a nation, their determination, proactivity and unanimous demand may force the parliament to start reforms. Today it is clear to all of us that what the state does is protect its citizens from wrongdoers that want to harm people's lives, their health, dignity and property. However, there is no effective and reliable protection from political villains. In truth, it should not only be the same but even better and more reliable than the protection from crime.

Giovani Sartori,[11] Jan-Erik Lane,[12] David Held[13] and many other authors referenced in this book have thoroughly analyzed the constitutions of many democratic countries and their influence on state government, they have also detected their variations and democratic anomalies, so we will try to look for practical and easily attainable ways of dealing with the stated *flaws of* democracy in order for it to be able to ensure happier lives for the citizens of every country without going too deep into the theoretical and philosophical differences of the attitudes of these authors.

Below we shall list the *flaws that disrupt the harmony of* democracy in a state and that worsen the lives of people in order to reflect on what it is that we should do to avoid such problems in the future or even make some of them completely obsolete. In our opinion, these are the *flaws of* state government:

- responsibility for the actions of politicians or public officials for their decisions, especially the collegial ones that have caused harm to the people or the state, is not being enforced;
- state law does not enable sufficient measures for the protection of its citizens from political fraud and other types of political crime, whereas protection from violent crime is being enforced quite satisfactorily and used effectively;
- a large part of the electorate does not participate in elections, which results in distorted representation;
- many of the elected parliament or municipality officials and parties do not keep their pre-election promises;

11 G. Sartori, Comparative Constitutional Engineering: An inquiry into Structures, Incentives and Outcomes.

12 J.E. Lane, Constitutions and Political Theory, chapter 11.

13 D. Held, Models of Democracy, chapters 9 and 10.

- criminals fight to get into government during elections in order to seek immunity from prosecution;
- parties running for election do not have enough qualified candidates to fill the responsible positions;
- parties that are not able or qualified to take part in state government are launched right before the elections;
- celebrities that are not qualified or suitable for parliamentary work are asked to become members of parties right before the elections;
- some parties use authoritarian rather than democratic means of internal administration;

We have listed the main f*laws of* democracy that disrupt the political lives of some states the most, and that is why we must examine the causes of these f*laws closer and try to find rational ways and measures to remove them, and if it is not possible to completely remove them – then at least minimize their influence on the political lives of these* states.

Having looked through these f*laws, we should be able to make a conclusion that every single one of them has more or less to do with the deficit of* responsibility of politicians and other political officials, and that is why we set ourselves the task of finding ways and measures to enforce the responsibility of every official in order to implement the principle of correlation of duties, rights and responsibilities in the state so it would become a state of responsible democracy.

3 Representation and Responsibility

In real life, the relationship between the representatives elected to the parliament or the municipalities and the citizens who elected them are complex and when poorly regulated or abused, give rise to the *flaws of* democracy. This is why we must dedicate ourselves to analyzing them.

The very essence of representation is that the elected individual (the representative) acts on the behalf of the person being represented, in his name and in his interests. That means that the representative has to enact the will of those he represents and be duly responsible for it. If the representative does something that is contrary to the will of the individual he represents, can we call such a person a representative? Definitely not! In this case, this individual will be acting on the behalf of somebody else, but not the person he was supposed to represent. An authorized person may only be called a representative as long as he is abiding by the will and defending the interests of the individual he represents. In order for the representative not to stray from acting contrary to the will of the person he represents, they draw up an agreement on a certain set of terms. Such an agreement defines the duties and rights of both sides, as well as any other conditions which determine the control of agreement performance, in other words – the control of the actions of both contracting parties, as well as the responsibility of non-compliance with the agreement.

Many countries have adopted the practice of the free mandate – one where having gotten over the election threshold and received a free mandate an individual can act based on his own conscience, of course, providing they do not violate the state constitution and the law. And if the conscience of this individual happens to be "handicapped", he may sometimes work against the will and the interests of the people who have elected him and will not feel the slightest bit responsible for it. That is why there is another opinion among constitutional law theoreticians which argues that the electorate is not really being represented unless the actions of the representative depend on their will, their needs or their wishes, and that is why they propose the use of an imperative mandate rather than a free mandate.[14] J.J. Rousseau has also expressed similar attitudes by claiming that the so-called representative institutions only impose the will of certain individuals on society, and yet there is no guarantee or even any likelihood that it would match the will of the people.[15]

The theory of social contract states that lawful authority is the result of an agreement among free individuals in their own free will. It sprang from the moral theory of St. Augustine in which he consolidated a strong bond between consent and free will. Thomas Hobbes – a famous English

14 The Blackwell Encyclopaedia of Political Thought, chapter "Representation".

15 J.J. Rousseau, The Social Contract and Other Later Political Writings.

philosopher who has also given a great deal of thought to the theory of social contract – has stated that the rights of a sovereign come from the consent of each of the people who shall be ruled by him.[16] In the research of the idea of social contract, J.J. Rousseau has written that every person is born free and is his own master, and nobody can enslave him by any means without his own consent. Immanuel Kant claimed that all rightful *laws should be such that allow rational human beings to consent to them.*[17] The rise of utilitarianism at the beginning of the 19th century has overshadowed the idea of social contract, but in the second half of the 20th century John Rawls substantiated the principles of justice (that a just society comes from voluntary cooperation) and gave impetus to the revival of the theory of social contract.[18]

According to the main idea of social contract, in representative democracy, individuals don't just accept the constitution by their own free will, but, in accordance with the provisions of the constitution, they also give authority to the representatives that they have chosen through democratic election, who then act in the name of the whole nation.

The constitutions of most democratic states have a provision which states that sovereignty belongs to the nation. Let's dismiss the cases of bribing voters and other instances of political fraud that regrettably still come up more often in the political practice of certain countries, and less so in the practice of other ones, and consider the voters' choice as it should be, were it in accordance with the principles of democracy.

16 T. Hobbes, Elements of Law.

17 I. Kant, Political Writings.

18 J. Rawls, A Theory of Justice.

When choosing the candidate or the electoral register to vote for, a voter should consider the ideological point of view of the candidate or the party (which can be understood from their political program), or to put it simply – their election promises, and give their vote to the party or the individual that best matches the interests or expectations of the voter. With this in mind, we come to the conclusion that at the time of the election an agreement between the voters and the candidate is made, on the basis of which the candidate acquires the authority to represent the voters who have elected him, and not just to work in his own best interests, which is quite often the case. Having noted that the constitutions of many countries state that when in their office, the members of the parliament should follow the constitution of the state and the *laws, and should work in the interests of the country according to their own conscience and cannot be restricted by any mandates, we should also note that they "shouldn't be restricted by mandates" only in the case of having followed all the aforementioned conditions, acting in accordance with the* constitution and working in the interests of the state being among them, as opposed to working only in their own interests.

The idea of granting legislative immunity is to allow members of the parliament to be able to do important government work without interruptions, provided that there are no serious grounds for it. But there are cases when legislative immunity becomes an instrument for malicious deeds. For example, there are cases of immunity being used as a means of protection for individuals who have committed a crime, but who have also found their way to parliament in order to avoid penalty. That is why this form of protection should be abolished.

On the other hand, although it is established in the constitutions of many countries that a member of the parliament cannot be prosecuted or otherwise have his freedom restricted without the assent of the parliament, some constitutions have exceptions for this, for example: parliament members in Austria[19] may be prosecuted for a criminal offence without the assent of the parliament, if the crime in question is not connected with their political work; in Belgium immunity is only guaranteed during the parliamentary session[20]; in Germany exclusions to immunity

19 **Constitution of Austria.**

Article 57.

2) The members of the National Council may on the ground of a criminal offence – the case of apprehension in the act of committing a crime excepted – be arrested only with the consent of the National Council. Domiciliary visitations of National Council members likewise require the National Council's consent.

3) Legal action on the ground of a criminal offence may otherwise without the National Council's consent be taken against members of the National Council only if it is manifestly not connected with the political activity of the member in question. The authority concerned must however seek a decision by the National Council on the existence of such a connection if the member in question or a third of the members belonging to the Standing Committee entrusted with these matters so demands. Every act of legal process shall in the case of such a demand immediately cease or be discontinued.

20 **The Belgian Constitution.**

Article 59.

Except in the case of a flagrant offence, no member of either House may, during a session and in criminal matters, be directly referred or summoned before a court or be arrested, except with the authorisation of the House of which he is a member.

Except in the case of a flagrant offence, coercive measures requiring the intervention of a judge cannot, during a session and in criminal matters, be instituted against a member of either House, except by the first President of the appeal court at the request of the competent judge. This decision is to be communicated to the President of the House concerned.

All searches or seizures executed by virtue of the preceding paragraph can be performed only in the presence of the President of the House concerned or a member appointed by him.

During the session, only the officers of the public prosecutor's office and competent officers may institute criminal proceedings against a member of either House.

The member concerned of either House may at any stage of the judicial enquiry request during a session and in criminal matters that the House of which he is a member suspend proceedings. To grant this request, the House concerned must decide by a majority of two thirds of the votes cast.

Detention of a member of either House or his prosecution before a court is suspended during the session if the House of which he is a member so requests.

include being caught at the scene of crime or one day after the crime[21] has been committed; the Japanese constitution states that except for cases not specified by the law, members of the parliament cannot be arrested during the session,[22] in France the penalties are not given by the whole parliament, but only by the parliament bureau which the member belongs to,[23] and in the USA senators and representatives have the right of immunity at all times except when tried for the crimes of treason, felony or public nuisance.[24] Some constitutions state that the general procedure of prosecution can be applied to a member of the

---

21 **Basic Law for the Federal Republic of Germany.**

Article 46 [Immunities of Members]

2) At no time may a Member be subjected to court proceedings or disciplinary action or otherwise called to account outside the Bundestag for a vote cast or for any speech or debate in the Bundestag or in any of its committees. This provision shall not apply to defamatory insults.

3) A Member may not be called to account or arrested for a punishable offence without permission of the Bundestag, unless he is apprehended while committing the offence or in the course of the following day.

22 **Constitution of Japan.**

Article 50:

Except in cases as provided for by law, members of both Houses shall be exempt from apprehension while the Diet is in session, and any members apprehended before the opening of the session shall be freed during the term of the session upon demand of the House.

23 **Constitution of France.**

Article 26.

No Member of Parliament shall be prosecuted, investigated, arrested, detained or tried in respect of opinions expressed or votes cast in the performance of his official duties.

No Member of Parliament shall be arrested for a serious crime or other major offence, nor shall he be subjected to any other custodial or semi-custodial measure, without the authorization of the Bureau of the House of which he is a member. Such authorization shall not be required in the case of a serious crime or other major offence committed *flagrante delicto* or when a conviction has become final.

24 **Constitution of the USA.**

Article 1.

Section 6

Compensation. The Senators and Representatives shall receive a Compensation for their Services, to be ascertained by Law, and paid out of the Treasury of the United States. They shall in all Cases, except Treason, Felony and Breach of the Peace, be privileged from Arrest during their Attendance at the Session of their respective Houses, and in going to and returning from the same; and for any Speech or Debate in either House, they shall not be questioned in any other Place.

parliament for personal insult or slander, and some of them specify actions committed before being elected as exceptions to immunity. That means that the legislative immunity of a parliament member is not absolute. And that is why we can speculate that this immunity should be limited in other special cases as well. It is important to note that the Swiss Confederation does not provide any immunity to its parliament members at all.

Considering the fact that changing a constitution that is valid at the moment might be quite complicated in any country, it is still possible to ensure responsibility of individual parliament members to their voters by enforcing a universal system of election promise monitoring, even if the constitutional right to legislative immunity for parliament members remains valid. We will refer to this in more detail in the chapter about election reform.

In certain countries if a member changes his parliamentary faction the event is seen as endangering the principles of democracy and even the integrity of statehood. In order to put a stop to this, the outrage of society or moral persuasion proves to be insufficient, and that is efforts to find more effective legal measures have to be made. Who can deny that a member elected through a party list and yet leaving it to join the faction of another party breaks his election promises and is acting dishonestly, breaks his pledge and should lose his right to represent the voters who gave him the mandate? The constitution of Portugal,[25] as

---

25 **Constitution of the Portuguese Republic.**

Article 160. (Loss and resignation of seat)

1. Members shall lose their seat in the event that:
   a) They become subject to any of the disqualifications or incompatibilities laid down by law;
   b) They do not take up their seat in the Assembly, or they exceed the number of absences laid down by the Rules of Procedure;
   c) They register as members of a party other than that for which they stood for

well as the constitution of India provide that a member of the parliament who has left the party through which he has been elected must lose his mandate.

Exceptions to this rule can include cases such as the member being elected without the help of the party, also when the party fails to deliver what it has promised before the election or does not comply with its own program, and the member wants to remain true to the promises he has given his voters and wants to protest against the agenda of the party that put him in the parliament. In this case, he should be given a chance to prove his entitlement in trial and the responsibility for the actions should be taken by the party that has let down its voters.

If an order like that were to be established, the fulfillment of election promises would have to be supervised. This would prevent political migrants who betray their voters for the sake of an office or other interests of their own from coming into existence. On the other hand, parties would also be forced to stick to their programs, which are seen by the voters as promises given to them. However, countries with deeply rooted traditions of democracy and a high-level political culture would not gain as much from this as post-Soviet democracies and some other countries would.

Party switchers and people who are disdainful of the will of their voters are plentiful in the municipalities as well. The enforcement of such an order in the municipal government as well as the parliament would strengthen party

---

election;

d) They are convicted by a court of any of the special crimes for which political officeholders may be held liable, which they commit in the exercise of their functions and for which they are sentenced to such loss, or they are convicted of participating in organisations that are racist or display a fascist ideology.

2. Members may resign their seat by means of a written declaration.

responsibility to their voters and prevent the members of local governments from running from party to party driven by dirty tricks. It would strengthen society's trust in their elected representatives.

4
PARTY REFORM

Most of the flaws listed in the second chapter of this book are connected to the work of political parties, so in order to make state governance more effective we must give our undivided attention to the fundamental reform of parties.

THE DEFORMATION OF PARTIES

We can assume that parties were not flawless in times past either if we look at the works of the Earl of Halifax, an English writer and politician who deemed political parties to be a sort of a plot against the remaining part of the nation as early as the second half of the 17th century. Critique of political parties can be found in the works of other political researchers of the past, as well as today. But, without going too deeply into the past, right now the relevance of the analysis of party influence on the life of the state can be proven by the deterioration of the attitude towards parties in most countries and the fact that right now a lot of parties receive a good deal of criticism. This can be seen by the decreased number of party members among the citizens of the whole country, as well as the decreasing rate of participation in state or municipal elections in the countries where voting is not mandatory.[26]

---

26 Voting is currently mandatory in: Argentina, Australia, Belgium, Bolivia, Brazil, Chile, The Dominican Republic, Egypt, Equador, Fiji, Gabon, Greece,

The results of various sociological research studies show that the trust people express in parties is minimal. There are countries where the people's trust of the parties is barely a few percent. This shows that politicians are not trusted there anymore and even the word 'politics' has become something mystical and connected with dark deeds. There are also countries where people express the same opinion about all parties – the good ones as well as the worst ones – they think of them almost as criminal gangs.

Analysis of the parliamentary work of many countries shows that in some of them a new parliament is not productive for the first 2-3 months – until the newly elected members "graduate the primary school" of legislation. Cases of when the position of a minister remains open for up to two months because the party couldn't find a suitable candidate are quite common. And sometimes even if the right candidate is found he still has to go through the "primary education of special governance". This often happens after the new head of a large government institution has been appointed as well. In conditions such as these the state government system becomes a system of education for political officials during a certain period after the election instead of having the new officials start their work right away. This urges us to look deeper into finding ways to avoid these situations.

If we were to look through newspapers and magazines, watch some TV and listen to the radio, we would surely hear a lot of well-grounded suggestions for improving the political life of every country, as well as some ungrounded ones, too. There would even be suggestions to bid democracy farewell,

---

Guatemala, Honduras, Cyprus, Costa Rica, Liechtenstein, Luxembourg, Mexico, Paraguay, Singapore, Thailand, Turkey and Uruguay.

to dismantle the parties. That they are allegedly useless, there are too many of them, they should not be funded by the state, that party election candidate lists should be withdrawn, etc. Having heard such suggestions, one starts to question which of these radical ideas come from actual thought and which are based on straight emotion. If we were to look at this issue in more detail in countries which are ruled by military juntas that have gained power in military coups and then subsequently banned all the parties in the state, as well as in countries which are dominated by a single party - a good example of this right now would be North Korea, it is the little people who are being oppressed the most. So we have to answer this question - is there a single democratic state that does not have any parties whatsoever? It is very unlikely that we would find such a state. We might not agree with the radical assessment of parties by the media, but we must agree with the importance of parties in today's democracy and set ourselves the task that instead of dismantling them or trying to create new ones, we will try to create a legal environment in which there would simply be no place for parties that look like political cartoons and all political organizations would become real parties that have the trust of society.

The Necessity for Party Reform

Political life must change in order not to become an anachronism and adapt to the changing public environment which in today's context can also be called an information society, not only because we have listed what in our opinion are the most important flaws of democracy and are willing to discuss several ways to get rid of them, but also because of the fact that in today's world technology changes the pace of human lives in so many unimaginable ways. These are all reasons why democracy needs change as well. Winston Churchill said that democracy is the worst form of government, except for all the others. The same can be said about parties as well. It is unlikely that we could find a better social structure able to choose and educate good politicians, who would not be disconnected from society and the nation, who could rule a country competently by following the principles of democracy. Fundamentally, such a structure can be a political party, no matter whether it is called a union, an alliance, a movement, a front, a move and so on. Unfortunately, at this time there are many parties that do not comply with the requirements stated above or cannot cope with the functions of a real political party. On the other hand, the people of most countries mostly associate the flaws of democracy with political parties, and that is why the imperfections of party activities must be examined in detail and ways to remove them must be found. That is yet another argument as to why reformation of state politics must begin with party reform.

Giovanni Sartori, one of the professors most quoted by political scientists, known widely as an expert on parties, election systems and democracy who has analyzed many state constitutions and the work of their parliaments in depth, stresses that no parliamentary democracy can function well if there are no parliamentary fit parties,[27] in other words – organizations that are integral and disciplined. Because of past failures, long standing and experience in politics, as well as the consequent drive connected to it, such parties have socialized into effective groups which are able to identify well, this being a prerequisite for an efficient parliament. Sartori sums up that it is always external violence and contamination that motivates an unstructured party system to become a structured one.

27 Sartori G., Comparative Constitutional Engineering: An inquiry into Structures, Incentives and Outcomes. 2nd ed. (1997)

It is unclear how much time would have to pass in order for the needed contamination to arise, considering the political environments of the countries in which democracy seems to function without major impediment, such as Switzerland. So in order to achieve the prompt and effective influence of parliamentary democracy on the lives of state citizens, there is no other way than to resort to legislative violence within the limits of the constitution, which would make parties integral, disciplined and capable.

In our opinion, in order for political parties to be able to do their work properly, they would have to be put into certain legal bounds that would not allow them to deviate from the path of virtue and help them avoid the influence of destructive forces. All of that necessitates the need for party reform, which we will discuss next.

If we want to achieve the improvement of human lives, superficial fixes of the law will hardly change the very essence of party work and society's opinion of the political environment and parties as one of the main elements of state politics, although this path should also not be rejected. In our opinion, a radical but well-grounded party reform is especially needed in the countries where society views political parties negatively.

A New View of Political Party

Let's think about what a party should really be like in order to adhere to the norms of democratic life. If we want a democracy to function reliably, to be trusted by its citizens and for politics to be an art worthy of the respect of society, we need properly adjusted and well-regulated political party activities. Legal regulations are needed in order to prevent abuse of authority and the emergence of various political criminals or people who are not suitable for such work because of their different reasons for seeking public office. We will stress again that normally a state strives to protect the lives, health, dignity and safety of its citizens and guests, as well as their property from criminal acts by every legally justified means available. And yet, most commonly there is no citizen protection from political fraud or individuals who cannot deal with government work. That means that as long as we consider "Justitia est fundamentum regnorum" ("Justice is Fundamental to Reign") to be correct, this anachronism has to go. Society must be legally protected from political criminals and the politically disabled.

Everybody knows that state government is demanding and complicated work, no matter which level of it we look at, and it can only be done satisfactorily by individuals who are duly educated and qualified, and when it comes to Lenin's idea of "every cook being able to run a state" – things like that should be considered political illiteracy. It is typical that individuals who want to obtain authority at any cost and yet aren't able to fully exploit all the facilities of it will usually resort to all sorts of violence, sometimes even psychological terror.

In order for a democratic state government to accomplish its functions in a qualified way, it needs to have a group of individuals that is well enough prepared to rule a country and yet is not alienated from the masses and not part of a privileged ruling class. This can be accomplished with a party system that works within certain legal bounds that comply with the principles of democracy.

The fundamental lawful way of gaining authority in a democratic system can only entail political parties. An individual joins a party for whatever reasons. If this individual expresses himself actively in party work, is good at socializing with others and maintains good relationships with his colleagues, he eventually receives a position in office. If he is diligent in holding his office, he might be elected to some representative position in the party or he might even be included in the party list for the local municipality candidates. This is the fundamental screening that takes place inside the party for people who are proactive, know how to socialize well and have a certain level of charisma. This is how the party elite is formed. If this party does well in an election, the elite members might become elected politicians. At least, that is how it should be – a modern party should not only be able to prepare its members for active participation in state government, but also cultivate a team of all sorts of leaders that could rule a state and its component parts competently. In our opinion, all this should be possible for a party with a clearly defined ideological direction in its program, a clear economic orientation, a stable scale of values, a knowledge of how to govern its inside processes according to democratic principles and an ability to take part in parliamentary activities in a straight-forward manner because its members know how to follow party disciplines.

Democracy in a Party

Conducting internal party policies in a democratic way is very important to a healthy democratic environment of a state. Unfortunately, the analysis of internal proceedings in parties shows that not all of them follow this order. Of course, there are parties that go back for years and years, and those are usually the ones with well-established internal traditions and their flaws in this regard are less obvious. Unfortunately, our observations show that there are quite a few deviations from the norm in the functioning of newly established parties. Of course, flaws can be detected even in parties of long-standing. Sartori stresses that in Brazil, for example, politicians think of their parties as '*partido de alugel*' – something on lease.[28] They are prone to switching parties often, they often vote against party lines and do not bother to comply with any party discipline, claiming that nobody should interfere with their freedom of representing their district the way they think best.

There are also parties whose initiator or leader thinks of himself as some sort of a feudal lord, surrounded by his toadying vassals, arrogant and displeased with any other opinion than his own, and the order of such parties often brings to mind an authoritarian regime, if not straight-forward dictatorship. Individuals who gain office in the parliament or municipalities through parties like these often have no experience or the ability to work in a democratic environment, so they often try to bring "the feudal spirit" which is based on violence and force back to fractions, committees and other government institutions. That puts a state with such parties in authority in danger of becoming totalitarian.

We can identify four principal notions in internal party policies that put it in danger of becoming authoritarian:

1) the working preferences of the leader;
2) the way in which meetings are held;
3) breaking the one vote per person principle;
4) for countries where a proportional election system is used – the order of drawing up election candidate lists and the way they are used.

28 Sartori G., Comparative Constitutional Engineering: An inquiry into Structures, Incentives and Outcomes. 2nd ed., 1997

The working preferences of the leader in great part depend on his weak preparation and knowledge of **management**, also on his abilities in state **governance** and his knowledge of social psychology. Even though such leaders often think that good results can be obtained by motivating their workers financially, they usually do not have the resources for it. They do not possess the whole arsenal of knowledge for manipulating people effectively, and so only resort to violence and force, sometimes even psychological terror. Every individual who has a different opinion, especially if it is an opposing one, makes such leaders think that they are their biggest enemy and they try to get rid of them by any means available. This is the way the surrounding environment selectively changes to one comprised mostly of people playing up to the leader, ones who agree with his every decision, even when they are his worst. This threatens the whole party as well as the leader's career and reinforces his belief that the most effective way of ruling is through force and violence, which in turn leads to an authoritarian leadership.

The way in which meetings are held. Fundamentally, party meetings should be held in order to clear up relevant issues, to find compromises to clashing opinions, to come to unanimous decisions about future actions. Of course, this can only be achieved through a thorough and honest discussion. The democratic spirit fails when meetings are conducted in a bad way, policies are not complied with, the higher officials control who gets a say and who doesn't. In this way the lackeys get to talk first and speak for a long time, and after that even those who put their names down to speak do not have enough time left to say anything of consequence. Resolutions and other decisions are usually made without thorough discussion and voting.

Voting. Voting is often abused in meetings. It must be mentioned that voting can be the means of legitimizing the resolutions of a meeting or a session, but it cannot remove the disagreements that cause conflicts and solve outstanding problems. It is not good for a conflict to stay unresolved and bottled up.

On the other hand, when making any decision at any level whatsoever, the principle of an open vote should be kept given that no law or regulation demands the opposite. However, if at least one individual with the right to vote demands it, a decision should be reached through a secret vote.

It is also not good when party assembly decisions, the choice of party leaders among them, are reached through the so-called "common agreement". Many party members as well as department leaders don't know the norm that is applicable to legal entities in certain countries which claims that when a poll is conducted and specific votes aren't counted, the voting must be repeated if at least one member opposes the decision, or even if they know it - they still ignore it completely. If the voting is repeated, the result of the first poll becomes legally invalid.

In many Western democracies the chairman usually abstains from voting in order to allow all other voters to choose without influence and thus making his lackeys cast votes based on their own opinion as well. The chairman only votes in the case of equal vote distribution. Then his vote is the casting vote - this helps keep the one vote per person principle. This is even stated in the Irish constitution (art. 15, 11.1 and 11.2[29]).

---

29 **Constitution of Ireland.**
Article 15. Part 11.

What is the function of this order? When there are two conflicting and opposing opinions in a party or a division and the chairman chooses one of them, the other side remains unsatisfied with both the results of the vote and the chairman himself. The disagreement remains, and this can lead both to conflict and the break-up of the party. When the chairman abstains from voting in a situation like this, none of the conflicting sides know his opinion, and so he is able to remain neutral and can function as a mediator who clears up the intricacies of the matter from both sides and can find a compromise. In this way he also solidifies his own status thanks to his authority, and not through sheer force or violence.

The order of drawing up election candidate lists and the way they are used. In the proportional system of election authoritarianism is allowed to thrive when candidate lists are drawn up by the party command only without adhering to the principles of democracy. This happens even faster when party members are encouraged to kowtow to the leaders, and when an individual has no hope of getting onto the list if he has ever expressed an opposing opinion to the leadership. When the chairperson feels unsure of his position, he might include certain individuals higher on the list simply in order to have a backing of sorts. Those who want to flatter the leadership often encourage an authoritarian atmosphere in a party this way without even being aware of it.

1 All questions in each House shall, save as otherwise provided by this Constitution, be determined by a majority of the votes of the members present and voting other than the Chairman or presiding member.

2 The Chairman or presiding member shall have and exercise a casting vote in the case of an equality of votes.

3 The number of members necessary to constitute a meeting of either House for the exercise of its powers shall be determined by its standing orders.

In proportional representation election systems where a rating system is enforced and is the main condition of being at a certain spot in the candidate list, this problem does not come up, provided that the voters understand the meaning of the rating system and use it well. Such systems are close to plurality voting systems because they give the right to vote for specific individuals. In order for a system such as this to be legalized, there must be a provision in the parliament election law that the number of mandates a party obtains is determined by the number of ballots, and the position in a candidate list is determined solely by the votes rating.

The Creation of New and Responsible Parties

In order to protect society from criminals burrowing their way into government, certain safety measures, such as requirements for the creation of parties and their activities, are needed to help them function in a way that is beneficial to society. If a party is given broad autonomy in its actions, it might be in danger of being exploited by individuals unprepared for ruling a state or members of organized crime in the worst possible case.

If we want to build a completely new concept, in our case – a model of an ideal party, we must first deny the current situation, as happens in any creative process, in order to free our minds completely from the stereotypes, traditions, laws or other limitations it already possesses. Having done that, we must formulate the mission of the party – one that clarifies what it is needed for – its purpose.

The main mission of the party should aim for the betterment of people's lives and the unification of the whole nation. There are many ways to achieve the improvement of citizen's lives, depending on the party ideology. The aim of parties being "to win the election and form a government", as defined in some textbooks, should be deemed as an inaccuracy and therefore it is sometimes quite accurately paraphrased by the opposition as "get your snout in the trough". Fundamentally, winning an election and forming a government is only a secondary goal, rather a condition that should be fulfilled in order to carry out the party mission – making reforms and improving the lives of the citizens.

Being in opposition does not grant a party the power to make reforms, but it should also perform a positive role: stressing the errors of the ruling majority and giving constructive suggestions instead of simply blindly criticizing it. So an opposing party can also have the same aim – raising the level of citizens' well-being. A party in opposition with such a mission should back those decisions of the majority that in their opinion do lead the state towards the improvement of citizens' lives.

A party is a political organization – meaning, it is connected to the rule of the state. So, one of its main tasks should be preparing its members to rule a state competently (both at the governmental and municipal level) and at the same time – singling out and educating political leaders. Most parties do not pay enough attention to this important task of staff preparation or even ignore it completely. That is why there are cases when many a new minister has to spend at least a few months learning to understand the current situation of the department, and during this time they are often led by the hand by more experienced officials and can make many mistakes which are then used by those same officials as a means of blackmail. As we have already mentioned, the process of preparation of responsible political party staff should be done in such a way that prevents a new minister from feeling like "a babe in the woods" and any candidate for ministerial office should go through the problems of the department beforehand and have submitted a reform project which would have already been accepted by the party leadership. In so doing ministers would feel at home in their office starting from day one and wouldn't let other officials "lead them by the hand". They would also be able to perform their ministerial duties productively and support the party line approved by voters by voting for the party. There would also be no disagreement between the ministry and the party leadership. This situation benefits society as well. Similar requirements should also be assumed for the parliament and municipality committee chairmen, as well as directly elected mayors and elders.

It is natural for parties to assume that "winning the election and forming a government" should be one of their goals, implying a necessity to be ready for it even before the election. That means that any party running for election should actually have a whole team of people instead of just one prepared to perform the duties of parliament members, municipality members, committee chairmen, ministers or mayors competently. Such jobs require a longer time span. That is why the parliament election law should define a certain amount of time for the said tasks, which would start at the moment of party registration and end when appointing candidates for the election. Such a provision would ensure the protection of the parliament from individuals unprepared for the work.

The political party laws in most countries define that when a party is being registered, it must present its policies, program and other documents. Requirements for party policies are listed in detail, but there are no specific requirements for a political program. Nevertheless, a party program should state what ideological direction the party has chosen and what the social classes whose interests it represents are. As we have mentioned, it should state the party mission, the main goals and the means of reaching them, as well as the ways the party will prepare its members for the competent rule of both the state and the local government. All these requirements should be defined in the law that regulates the forming of political parties.

Party Structure and Forming Government Bodies

Distortion of party activity, or, as we have previously called it, the flaws of distortion arise because of the corruption of internal party processes, party management among them. Keeping in mind that no process happens without the presence of a structure, we can say that a rational party body structure is needed to ensure protection from the dangers of harm done by the use of destructive practices. It is not the naming convention of this or that party body that is important as much as the clear regulation of its competences and responsibilities.

The most important body of a party is usually the assembly of members which includes all the members of the party or their representatives that take part in it according to all the accepted rules of representation. The assembly is summoned at certain intervals and establishes or dissolves a party, consolidates party regulations and the program, forms its authoritative bodies or audit commissions and makes other decisions of major importance. Usually, the assembly is summoned at intervals defined in the party regulations, normally every 2 to 3 years. In the intervals between party assemblies, the most important questions are solved by a council elected by the assembly, which is usually directed by a party chairman who is also elected by the assembly. The assembly and council decisions are implemented by the party administration (the council presidium) which is also directed by the party chairperson. The elected chairperson becomes both the leader of the council and the administration by default and does not have to be elected separately.

A definite date for the assembly is usually announced at least a month prior to it by the council, as well as the norms of the assembly and the planned resolution and document projects in order for the members to be able to familiarise themselves with the material beforehand and be able to express their opinion about them.

The assembly, being directed by the deputy (or deputies) of the chairperson, chooses a chairperson through a secret ballot[30] from at least two candidates, first of all having listened to everything that the chairman has to say and seen all the reports by the audit commission, having analyzed them and made certain decisions.

The assembly usually elects the party council. The list of possible candidates for the council usually includes party regional department representatives (one or more per department, depending on the party regulation norms) and a certain number – usually no more than 20 percent – of the council candidates that have been selected by the administration prior to the assembly. The ballot should enable a representative to cast a vote for every candidate separately. Of course, other ways of forming a council are acceptable as well.

30 **Constitution of the Portuguese Republic. (2005)**

Article 55, Part 3:

Trade unions shall be governed by the principles of democratic organization and management, to be based on periodic elections of their managing bodies by secret ballot, without the need for any authorization or homologation, and shall be founded on active worker participation in every aspect of trade union activity.

The party council elects the administration through voting for every candidate separately. Individuals who have received the least number of votes in the council election should not be allowed to be listed in the candidate list for the administration election. After that, the council elects deputies for the chairperson out of the chosen board members who are suggested as candidates by the party chairperson.

These requirements should be defined in both the party law and the party regulations. If the requirements for the formation of party administrative bodies and the election of the administration board were properly maintained, the democratic spirit inside the parties would be kept safe and internal party process flaws would be avoided.

Party Funding

The funding of political parties has to be strictly regulated by the law because it is quite common for political corruption to hide under the cloak of funding. There is a saying that goes like this – "He who pays the piper calls the tune". That means that if the citizens want parties to serve common honest people instead of the oligarchy, as is often the case in this wicked world, they must agree that they should be financed through the money of taxpayers instead of the oligarchy, too.

In order for parties to be able to survive lawfully (without the aid of dirty money) and perform their functions properly, they should be financed through:

1) membership fees;
2) party publication benefits;

3) state funding;
4) fixed donations by natural persons;
5) perhaps some other means of financing, the usage and sources of which must still be strictly regulated by law.

We know through experience that donations to political parties made by legal entities are often connected with one or other form of bribery or corruption, and that is why this form of funding should not be allowed or should at least be limited to a really small amount, for example, not any more than the sum of five minimum wages.

The maximum membership fee should be defined by the law and the monthly fee should not be larger than 1-2% of the established average monthly wage of the state in the previous year. That should eliminate the possibility of money laundering into the party fund through large membership fees, which does sometimes occur.

The law should regulate the order of party financing through benefits from party publications as well.

The limit for donations from natural persons should not be very high, for example, it should not be larger than the donor's salary for one month in the previous year. This would eliminate money laundering by natural persons.

We will discuss the suggested order of state funding through the national treasury in more detail. The best overseer for any activity is the consumer. The consumers of political produce – the state laws – are the citizens of the state. Many of these citizens are voters. We cannot think of the voters as "country bumpkins" that know no better – such a point of view in a democratic society should not only be condemned, but also punished. Voters can be the best judges of politicians' actions and the best dividers of political party funds. Instead of state officials doing the job, as is usually the case in certain states, the voters should have the right to distribute a certain percentage of their income tax (e.g. 1%) to any officially registered party. Such an allocation of a certain percentage of their income tax would not cost the taxpayers anything and would have certain other advantages. It would strengthen the ties between political forces and non-party individuals, especially working (tax-paying) citizens and would give a source of funding to non-parliamentary parties. With this order in action, the party administration would encourage its members to ask their co-workers, neighbors, relatives and other acquaintances to allocate a percentage of their income tax to the party. In turn, these individuals would be able to express their opinions to the party. This means that intensive collaboration would begin between the party members and the citizens and the party would know the opinions of citizens in more detail. It would also try to satisfy the needs of citizens. During this process the political environment of the state would renew itself because non-parliamentary parties would be able to function properly by receiving more attention from society.

If we want taxpayers to allocate certain budget amounts to political parties, a ratio must be applied to the 1% of income tax, the size of which would be defined every year by the ministry, depending on the sum allocated in the budget especially for the parties and the funds which constitute 1% of the income tax. For example, if the number that makes up 1% of the income tax is smaller than the sum allocated in the budget for the given year, this ratio should be bigger than 1, and if it is bigger – the ratio should be smaller than 1.

This is the only system of party funding that would not cause the state to sacrifice any funds, but in turn would change the situation fundamentally. Another plus of this method of funding is the ability to control and dissolve fake parties that only exist legally. Only parties that have been supported by a certain legally defined minimum number of individuals with 1% of their income tax should be deemed ‘recognized by society’ and be able to avoid an audit.

With the aim of dissolving parties that receive no support from the society, it should perhaps be defined that a party which has not been supported by the required number of individuals should be allowed to present a list of retired individuals (individuals who have no insured income) to cover the number by which it falls short, and if the party fails to do this, it would be dissolved. It is predictable that the number of parties would shrink significantly.

If we want to prevent the existence of party funding by illegitimate means, the exceptional discounts for party advertising material in the media should also be viewed as a type of bribery.

Election Reform

As observation shows, there are quite a lot of individuals unprepared or unsuited for legislative work who still manage to make their way into parliament in certain countries. We cannot deny that an individual with an academic background of political sciences in the government would be a negative phenomenon. However, if an order similar to the one that Plato has reasoned about were to be enforced (that is, a special educational facility would prepare future politicians who would then be the only ones with the right to work in the state government), a democratic system would be more than doubtful or even impossible. A distinct class of political officials, remote from real life, would develop, and it would be no different from a totalitarian regime that has a hold on the government, which is often the case after a coup.

Requirements for Candidates

Everybody knows that an athlete does not have the right to perform an appendectomy instead of a certified medical doctor, no matter how much he is admired. A celebrity would also not be allowed to pilot an airplane on his own. A world-class pilot would not be given the right to drive a car if he didn't have a driver's license. However, phenomena that could be called none other than anomalies simply thrive in the political world. Voters gladly give their votes to well-known people who are gifted in their areas of expertise: sports stars, famous singers, acclaimed writers, TV celebrities. Most of the time the voters do not consider that even though that person is highly skilled in his own field, he has no experience in politics or legislation. If this person is well-known in his area of work, it's because he has dedicated his life to it – his life was made up of rehearsals or training. The voters also do not consider that parliamentary work might not “agree with this person”, that he has simply been coaxed into signing up for the party candidate list, and yet he is still voted for. And it is only because he is a famous person. This phenomenon itself is not inherently bad. The worst thing in this is that some parties will start recruiting celebrities to join them right before the election. This is how an ‘odd one out’ appears among experienced parliament members. Maybe it is not so bad if it is just one person, but if there are more than one? This means that it is not as important to have a ‘new face’, as the voters often demand it, what matters is who the ‘new face’ is and what hides behind it. This phenomenon could be avoided if a rule were to be defined, stating that a candidate list can only include party members who have at least one year of experience of working with the party. This regulation would prevent pre-election recruitment of celebrities to political party lists.

The experience of forming parliaments shows that parties established right before an election do not bring any good to the political environment either. Such parties, having captivated the voters with the idea that politics needs new faces, sometimes achieve a striking victory. This is especially the case if such a party has celebrities who know how to communicate with the voters, who in turn long for new faces. Most commonly, such parties do not have sound ideological foundations to unify their members, and that is why their further actions cannot be predicted. Such parties tend to have their members switching fractions the most. Within such disorder, the representatives often do not even know who it is they represent anymore, and we cannot even begin to speak of any responsibility to their voters.

It is also quite typical for people to think that celebrities or even they themselves would be able to rule the country better than qualified politicians. That is why individuals unprepared or unsuited for legislative work end up being elected to parliament. Sometimes there are even criminal characters, women with a shady past, well-known and admired magnates of the entertainment industry among the elected representatives, who receive many votes. Although there are cases of such individuals being able to perform their duties to the state competently, most of the time such characters bring about so many problems that not even a whole term is enough to right the wrongs.

Our opponents refer to Ronald Reagan, former President of the United States as such an example. But many people do not know that he had previously worked in executive positions for many years. During his time in the military, he had earned the rank of Captain, had been elected as President of the Screen Actors Guild six times, and had served as Governor of the State of California between 1967 and 1975. That is why his experience in the area of state governance and his preparation for ruling a country was undeniable.

All of this shows that in order to protect the interests of society, legal measures that limit the access of individuals who are unsuitable or unprepared for legislative work to parliament should be taken. In order to encourage parties to prepare their members for competent state governance, a requirement should be defined in the parliament and municipality election laws that along with the election candidate list, the party should also present a list of individuals prepared and suitable to take the offices of ministers, parliament committee chairmen, and for municipality elections – the offices of council committee chairmen (for no less than 50% of the offices needed to be filled in the whole state). Then the voters would know the team of party members who would govern the state and it would be easier for them to decide on the party they would vote for. In connection with this, the political party and political organisation law must have a requirement which would state that the party is only allowed to register candidates for an election two years after its establishment. These two years would function as the span of time during which the party should gain enough approval from society and be able to prepare its members for competent state government.

In order for every voter to be able to acquaint themselves with the programs of all the parties running for election and choose the one that represents their interests the best, the election law should define that every election subject should present, along with the election registration forms, a shortened version of the program (often referred to as a manifest), no bigger than, for example, two pages long, which would state the definitive objectives (objects) that the party wants to accomplish during the term that is defined by law in the given state, the definite deadlines by which each objective needs to be fulfilled, as well as the intellectual and material resources needed in order for every task to be carried out, and also where these resources will be obtained. This would allow every voter to read the manifests of all the parties instead of just one or two, and choose the one that suits him best. Also, this would allow for the possibility of checking up on the election promises of the party after some time has passed.

The election law must also state that it should be mandatory for parties to publicly inform society of any changes to the election program commitments when forming a coalition.

Responsibility for Election Promises

Legal establishment of party election manifests in a certain form, detailing party responsibilities and their deadlines in a concise and clear way, also budgets and their sources, would allow for the constant supervision of the enactment of responsibilities. The institution that held the election should handle monitoring. Every parliament member should be given a personal website which would detail party responsibilities, or in the case of a plurality voting system, his own personal obligations and the voting results proportional to each obligation. A similar system should be used for party websites as well. Today's technology allows for the automatic monitoring of these obligations, using certain types of software. Of course, considering the independence of each parliament member, it should be possible to clarify on the webpage why the member has voted against or abstained from voting at all. All of the bills and other projects the parliament member has registered should be placed on this page as well. The monitoring system should be open to the public so that every voter can see the page of any parliament member or party. This order should guarantee the transparency of the work that parliament members and parties do, and also give the media a chance to reveal cases of political fraud and corruption.

The Accountability and Responsibility of Politicians and State Officials

A newly appointed or elected state or municipality chief officer with little experience often does not know which direction he should take in the administration of the institution he has just been put in charge of, and since the way of life is such that one should first take care of the tasks that are more pressing, and such tasks are plentiful in any institution, the chief officer is often overwhelmed by them, and there is no time left to solve the bigger problems.

The work of politicians and state officials should be done in order to bring prosperity to the nation, and that is why it should be mandatory for state and municipality officials to give reports to society regularly and after each term. Up till now, the state officials of most countries have used the increase of gross domestic product (GDP) as a measurement of their work results, and also GDP per capita. Fundamentally, GDP measures the value of all the products and services that all the citizens of the state generate, but it does not show the level of prosperity of the nation, and that is why using the GDP to measure the well-being of a state is not adequate. Theoretically, it is possible for the country's GDP to be the highest in the world, and yet it can still have the highest poverty rate. The well-being of a nation does not depend solely on GDP, but also on the way it is distributed.

For example, the GDP per capita of the United Arab Emirates (USD 49 700) is one of the highest in the world, but most of the country's GDP goes to the Sheikh families, and most of the other citizens starve. On the other hand, if production is increased, GDP increases as well, but that can cause more pollution and worsen the conditions of people's lives. Some African countries raise their GDP through reckless destruction of the forests and selling the wood, although that in turn increases the area of deserts, worsens the climate and destroys the foundations of the life of the nation.

Economic activity causes more pollution in general, so a growing GDP per capita may conceal the worsening health of the nation as well.

These days, the general well-being of a nation is usually expressed though a set of key indicators, the average wage, integrity and alienation in the society, the level of public safety, morbidity and the average life expectancy, healthy environment, means of education and improvement to name but a few. Naturally, GDP per capita can be used as one of the indicators of the well-being of a nation, but it cannot be the critical one.

The strategies of some democratic countries use the following indicators:

1) quality of life index;
2) happiness index;
3) index of democracy;
4) index of society integrity;
5) index of competitiveness;
6) globalization index.

In order for all the government officials, institution leaders, politicians and state officers to dedicate their work to the prosperity of the nation, certain criteria should be established by the law, which would oblige politicians and state officials to give regular accounts of their work to the nation and be responsible for the achievement of certain indicators based on certain criteria. The results of these accounts and their evaluation should be publicly accessible to every citizen on the websites of local and state governments.

Experience shows us that sometimes a mayor will become generous towards populist programs and get the municipality into debt, will not pay the due taxes for years and at the end of his term he will still be deemed a "good mayor". The mayor that succeeds him will face the demands of creditors, account arrest and financial paralysis of the municipality affairs starting on day one. Winning the name of a good mayor in these circumstances is very hard and might even prove impossible for the newcomer.

The proposed law should define the indicators of the work results for politicians and public officials, how the indicators should be publicized, the content of the reports and their regularity, order of evaluation, a reward system for those who did well and the way responsibility is handled when harm is done to the society and the state.

The control of the actions of parliament members with regard to their election promises has already been detailed in chapter 5.2, so we will not reiterate it, but we must note that the number of votes that each parliament member has not taken part in should be published by the Parliament Ethics Committee online, and no later than the 5th day of every month. A member of the parliament, like any other person who has put his personal and public interests in conflict, should not be presented for national distinction orders or a retirement plan.

The evaluation of the work of a Prime Minister. Every Prime Minister who has resigned from the office, regardless of the reason for the resignation, should present an account of his work to the parliament within a month of the resignation date. This account should consist of key indicators about conditions in the state when he took up office and the time he resigned:

- number of citizens (men and women) on January the 1st;
- number of births in the previous year;
- rate of unemployment in the past month;
- the average retirement pension in the past month;
- the average wage in the past month;
- social alienation in the previous year;
- the number of public staff in the past month;
- crime levels of the past year (per 10 000 citizens)
- GDP per capita in the previous year;
- gold reserves in the past month;
- international trade balance in the previous year;
- international debt in the previous month;
- national debt in the previous month;
- quality of life index in the previous year;
- happiness index in the previous year;
- democracy index in the previous year;
- society integrity index in the previous year;
- index of competitiveness in the previous year;
- globalization index in the previous year;

- poverty rate in the previous year.

The parliament should then evaluate the report. If the report were seen as a positive one, the Minister could then be put forward for a national honor award.

The evaluation of a Minister's work. Regardless of the reason for resignation, every minister should present an account of his time in office. This account should consist of key indicators about conditions when he took up office and the time he resigned. These key indicators should fall within the competences of the ministry. The minister should only be presented for national honor awards if his work has been evaluated positively by the parliament.

The responsibility of mayors. Regardless of the reason for resignation, every mayor should present an account of his time in office. This account should consist of key indicators about conditions when he took up office and the time he resigned:

- number of citizens (men and women) on January the 1st;
- number of births in the previous year;
- rate of unemployment in the past month;
- average retirement pension in the past month;
- average wage in the past month;
- social alienation in the previous year;
- number of municipal staff in the past month;
- crime levels of the past year (per 10 000 citizens);
- GDP per capita in the previous year;
- municipal debt in the previous year;
- quality of life index in the previous year;

- happiness index in the previous year;
- democracy index in the previous year;
- society integrity index in the previous year;
- poverty rate in the previous year;
- collected income-tax;
- municipal budget;
- percentage of paved roads;
- level of pollution in the city center in the previous month;
- quality of drinking water in the previous month;
- average price of central heating in the previous year.

The accountability of city council members. The members of city council should be responsible both morally and financially for their votes for certain decisions that have brought harm to the citizens or the state. Only those who have voted against a resolution, have not taken part in the vote or who have presented an objection in written form no later than a week after the vote, should be exempt.

Two-House Parliaments

The well-being of citizens depends on the way the state is ruled: there are no poor states, only states that are ruled poorly. The efficiency of state government is determined first of all by the quality of the state constitution, assuming it is being executed, and the parliament. There are cases when a comparatively good constitution is not executed, as in the case of the Soviet Union, but if the constitution itself is no good, then the probability of an efficient government in the state is very small.

The influence the parliament has over the state government is marked because if the parliament were to put a flawed law into action, all the other government institutions would follow suit with the repetition of this legal flaw. In countries which could be governed in a much better way, the opponents of the government sarcastically remark that the only reason the parliament passes bad laws which are not in accordance with the requirements of life and the society, have no perspective, do not evaluate the new social, economic or political conditions, is so that later on they would have a lot of work to do correcting or amending these laws. In other countries, the excuse that the former parliament has passed a lot of bad quality laws, and that is why the new parliament is forced to busy itself with fixing them, is popular, too. When internal and external conditions change, some of the laws have to undergo corrections. However, the fact that in some countries the parliament passes very few new or original laws, and some of the older laws are changed or appended at least two or three times each year, only shows the insufficiently perfected system of legislation.

Regardless of the real reasons for changing the laws, justifiable or not, the "obsession" with constant editing leads businessmen and other citizens to be uncertain about the future, distrustful of the government, expectant of another change in the law, which causes the enactment of it to be stalled and gives rise to legal nihilism, slowing down the economic and social growth of the state.

Legislation is regulated by the parliament statute, but we cannot expect that superficial legal changes through changing individual provisions in the statute would be able to fundamentally improve the legislation process. Superficiality in state governance does not usually remove the accumulated problems and sometimes even makes them worse. That is why we think that it is meaningful to speak of reforming the system of legislation.

States with an effective legislation system usually have a two-house parliament system. This is the case in the USA, Japan, Germany, France and many other countries, with Poland having both a parliament and a senate. Most countries in the European Union also have a two-house system, although the higher house can have different names in different countries: the Senate in Ireland, Belgium, Spain and Italy, The Federal Council in Austria, The Bundesrat in Germany (translated as "The Union Council"), The First House in the Netherlands (the lower house is called The Second House), and The House of Lords in Great Britain. The only remaining countries in the European Union that still have a single-chamber parliament are three monarchies – Denmark, Luxembourg and Sweden, and only two republics – Greece and Finland, if one does not count the post-soviet states. In Finland the function of the higher house is performed by the **Grand Committee**[31] which was established back in 1906. Without its assent, no law can see the light of day. This Committee is usually made up of 25 members and 9 deputies, all in all – 34 people. It is elected during the first session of every new parliament.

31 **Constitution of Finland.**

Section 35 - Committees of the Parliament.

For each electoral term, the Parliament appoints the **Grand Committee**, the Constitutional Law Committee, the Foreign, Affairs Committee, the Finance Committee, the Audit Committee and the other standing Committees provided in the Parliament's Rules of Procedure. In addition, the Parliament appoints Committees ad hoc for the preparation of, or inquiry into, a given matter. (596/2007, entry into force 1.6.2007)

The **Grand Committee** shall have twenty-five members. The Constitutional Law Committee, the Foreign Affairs Committee and the Finance Committee shall have at least seventeen members each. The other standing Committees shall have at least eleven members each. In addition, each Committee shall have the necessary number of alternate members.

A Committee has a quorum when at least two thirds of its members are present, unless a higher quorum has beenspecifically required for a given matter.

Section 50 - Public nature of parliamentary activity.

The plenary sessions of the Parliament are open to the public, unless the Parliament for a very weighty reason decides otherwise for a given matter. The Parliament publishes its papers, as provided in more detail in the Parliament's Rules of Procedure.

The meetings of Committees are not open to the public. However, a Committee may open its meeting to the public during the time when it is gathering information for the preparation of a matter.

The minutes and other related documents of the Committees shall be made available to the public, unless a Committee for a compelling reasondecides otherwise for a given matter.

The members of a Committee shall observe the level of confidentiality considered necessary by the Committee.

However, when considering matters relating to Finland's international relations or European Union affairs, the members of a Committee shall observe the level of confidentiality considered necessary by the Foreign Affairs Committee or the **Grand Committee** after having heard the

Even though Norway has a single-chamber parliament, when it first assembles, it is divided into two parts[32] and continues working as a two-house one. The parliament of Iceland functions in a similar manner.

Giovanni Sartori, whom we already know well, having analyzed the parliamentary practice of many countries in depth has proven the superiority of a two-house system compared to a single-chamber one.[33] Jan-Erik Lane, a political scientist and a famous advocate for new institutionalism, having analyzed the constitutions of many

---

opinion of the Government.

Section 72 - Consideration of a legislative proposal in the Parliament

Once the relevant report of the Committee preparing the matter has been issued, a legislative proposal is considered in two readings in a plenary session of the Parliament.

In the first reading of the legislative proposal, the report of the Committee is presented and debated, and a decision on the contents of the legislative proposal is made. In the second reading, which at the earliest takes place on the third day after the conclusion of the first reading, the Parliament decides whether the legislative proposal is accepted or rejected.

While the first reading is in progress, the legislative proposal may be referred to the Grand Committee for consideration.

More detailed provisions on the consideration of a legislative proposal are laid down in the Parliament's Rules of Procedure.

32 **Constitution of Norway.**

Article 73

The Storting nominates from among its Members one fourth to constitute the Lagting; the remaining three fourths constitute the Odelsting. This nomination shall take place at the first session of the Storting that assembles after a new General Election, whereafter the Lagting shall remain unchanged at all sessions of the Storting assembled after the same election, except insofar as any vacancy which may occur among its Members has to be filled by special nomination.

Each Ting holds its meetings separately and nominates its own President and Secretary. Neither Ting may hold a meeting unless at least half of its Members are present. However, Bills concerning amendments to the Constitution may not be dealt with unless at least two thirds of the Members of the Storting are present.

33 G. Sartori, chapter 12.1.

countries and their influence on the life of the states, has declared that bicameralism (a two-chamber parliament system) results in a higher level of citizen prosperity and smaller expenditure for the state.[34]

Among the smaller countries in Europe, it was Finland and Ireland that made the greatest advancements in the past few decades in terms of the well-being of their citizens. Although Ireland received a strong blow in 2008, due to the financial crisis, it has been able to cope with the hardship much more successfully than some other countries that have suffered at the same time. So perhaps we should look at the way these countries are governed and their legislative experience in more detail.

The area of the Republic of Ireland is 70 282 km². According to the data of 1994, it had a population of 3.6 million. Finland is much bigger - 337 000 km², and a population of - 5.5 million. In Ireland and Finland, the president is elected directly, by means of a secret ballot of citizens.

34 G. Sartori, chapter 12.1.

Article 18 of the Constitution of Ireland[35] defines that the state parliament is composed of two houses – the House of Representatives (the Dáil) and the Senate. Electing the members for the House of Representatives is not particularly different than for the elections of lower houses of other nations. But the formation of the Irish Senate is worth looking at. The Senate consists of 60 senators. Eleven of them are appointed by the prime minister, 6 are elected by

---

35 **Constitution of Ireland.**

Article 18.

1. Seanad ireann shall be composed of sixty members, of whom eleven shall be nominated embers and forty-nine shall be elected members.
2. A person to be eligible for membership of Seanad ireann must be eligible to become a member of DÆl ireann.
3. The nominated members of Seanad ireann shall be nominated, with their prior consent, by the Taoiseach who is appointed next after the re-assembly of DÆl ireann following the dissolution thereof which occasions the nomination of the said members.
4.
   1 The elected members of Seanad ireann shall be elected as follows:
      - i. Three shall be elected by the National University of Ireland.
      - ii. Three shall be elected by the University of Dublin.
      - iii. Forty-three shall be elected from panels of candidates constituted as hereinafter provided.

   2 Provision may be made by law for the election, on a franchise and in the manner to be provided by law, by one or more of the following institutions, namely:
      - i. the universities mentioned in subsection 1 of this section,
      - ii. any other institutions of higher education in the State, of so many members of Seanad ireann as may be fixed by law in substitution for an equal number of the members to be elected pursuant to paragraphs i and ii of the said subsection 1 .
      - iii. A member or members of Seanad ireann may be elected under this subsection by institutions grouped together or by a single institution.

   3 Nothing in this Article shall be invoked to prohibit the dissolution by law of a university entioned in subsection 1 of this section.
5. Every election of the elected members of Seanad ireann shall be held on the system of proportional representation by means of the single transferable vote, and by secret postal ballot.
6. The members of Seanad ireann to be elected by the Universities shall be elected on a franchise and in the manner to be provided by law.
7.
   1 Before each general election of the members of Seanad ireann to be elected from panels of candidates, five panels of candidates shall be formed in the manner provided by law containing respectively the names of persons having knowledge and practical experience of the following interests and services, namely:

the graduates of certain Irish universities; 3 by graduates of the National University of Ireland and 3 by graduates of the University of Dublin. The 43 other senators are elected by individuals from special panels of nominees (known as Vocational Panels) by an electorate consisting of the members of parliament, senators and local councilors. Only members of the legislature and other designated bodies are entitled to nominate. Each of the five panels consists of the individuals possessing special knowledge or experience in one of five specific fields: 1) culture and education, 2) agriculture and related practices, 3) formal and non-formal work, 4) industry and market trade, including banking,

---

i. National Language and Culture, Literature, Art, Education and such professional interests as may be defined by law for the purpose of this panel;
ii. Agriculture and allied interests, and Fisheries;
iii. Labour, whether organised or unorganised;
iv. Industry and Commerce, including banking, finance, accountancy, engineering and architecture;
v. Public Administration and social services, including voluntary social activities.

2 Not more than eleven and, subject to the provisions of Article 19 hereof, not less than five members of Seanad ireann shall be elected from any one panel.

8. A general election for Seanad ireann shall take place not later than ninety days after a dissolution of DÆil ireann, and the first meeting of Seanad ireann after the general election shall take place on a day to be fixed by the President on the advice of the Taoiseach.

9. Every member of Seanad ireann shall, unless he dies, resigns, or becomes disqualified, continue to hold office until the day before the polling day of the general election for Seanad ireann next held after his election or nomination.

10.

1 Subject to the foregoing 3 provisions of this Article elections of the elected members of Seanad ireann shall be regulated by law.

2 Casual vacancies in the number of the nominated members of Seanad ireann shall be filled by nomination by the Taoiseach with the prior consent of persons so nominated.

3 Casual vacancies in the number of the elected members of Seanad ireann shall be filled in the manner provided by law.

Article 19

Provision may be made by law for the direct election by any functional or vocational group or ssociation or council of so many members of Seanad ireann as may be fixed by such law in substitution for an equal number of the members to be elected from the corresponding panels of candidates constituted under Article 18 of this Constitution.

finance, accounting, engineering and architecture, 5) state government. A certain number of senators must be chosen from each category but there may be no less than 5 and no more than 11 members each. This means that the quality of the Irish government is determined by an alliance of politicians and scientists.

According to the constitution of certain countries, a law comes into effect only when the president of the republic signs it and officially declares it. Of course, generally, aside from only signing it and officially declaring it, the president also has the right of returning it to the parliament for another reading. This means that while the president has final control over the laws issued by parliament, he cannot physically do the job. In reality, this job is done by the president's advisers, whose offices are not considered constitutional. This means that following governmental logic, the work results of the parliament are monitored by non-constitutional staff. This collision would resolve itself if the parliament were divided into two houses. Then legislation would be a little slower, but its quality would be much higher.

In our opinion, the Senate, as in the case of Ireland, or the Grand Committee in Finland, should have 7-10 specialists from each of the five aforementioned branches of knowledge. Also, former presidents should have the right to become Senate members, if they so wish. Their experience would surely be beneficial to the state.

Citizens with a university education and practical experience of at least 10 years in one of the areas in question should be allowed to run for the Senate. They should be backed by university science councils, science academies, municipal associations, business associations, industry or law associations and other highly qualified professional organizations defined in the law. Candidates should also be able to run for election themselves, provided that they are current or former parliament members who have previously worked in the system for at least two terms. Senators would be chosen in a general election for a term of 8 years, with half of the Senate being replaced every 4 years.

If the parliament were to be divided into two houses, the general functions of the House of Representatives would not change fundamentally. They would still be held fully responsible for approval by the prime minister's office and the program of the government. At the same time, the Senate would sanction the declarations of war, issues of emergency situations, calls for mobilization or the use of armed forces inside and outside of the state, issued by the state president, and it would also approve or disapprove the amendments to the constitution and the laws that the house of representatives has issued. With a two-house parliamentary system, everyone with the right of legislation granted by the constitution would know that the bills issued would be analyzed in more detail, and thus would feel a commitment to issue better bills. Finally, a two-house parliamentary system is much less likely to be at the risk of corruption.

Presidential Dangers

According to constitutional law specialists, the most advanced and most democratic form of government is a democracy. In a democratic state, all the highest government bodies are elected, but there are cases when they can be chosen by members of parliament. For example, the parliament can elect the president. A republic can be either parliamentary or presidential, but in the practice of state government a middle-ground between these two extremities can be found as well, and this is generally called a semi-presidential republic.

Constitutional law historians consider that the parliamentary republic was formed through natural evolution,[36] and the presidential republic was an artificially crafted form of government. In short, in the parliamentary republic, the parliament represents the nation, issues laws and approves the budget, forms and controls the government, and so it is always clear that the majority forming the parliament is responsible for the enactment of the election promises. Of course, it is possible to have an unstable government if the parliamentary majority is divided. And when it comes to a presidential republic, the

36 It is thought that parliamentarism began with King Louis IX of France, who would regularly assemble a council for the most important questions of state. He then established a House of Court which was later renamed a parliament. At first, parliaments had representatives from the classes of large land owners, aristocrats and the clergy. In the 17-18th century, parliaments became the representation houses for the nation.

legislative government (the parliament) and the executive government (the president and the government) usually do not depend on one another, although this is not absolute. The president controls the parliament through signing or vetoing the laws it passes. The parliament can reject the president's veto through a qualified vote (usually as long as at least two thirds of the parliament vote against). The parliament has the right to approve the ministerial candidates. And yet, in a presidential republic the president has a lot of authority, and that is why it is very important to have a morally firm president. Most presidents of presidential republics, because of the lack of control by parliament, have used their authority to gain immeasurable weatlh at the price of the poverty of its citizens.

The World Bank and Transparency International have composed a list of the 10 most corrupt politicians who got their hands on their states' budgets over the past 40 years. Among them one can find:

1. **Haji Mohammad Suharto (Soeharto), Indonesia (1921 - 2008).**
Stole USD 15-35 billion. A veteran of the Indonesian National Revolution, a hero of the nation who ruled the state for 20 years (1968 to 1998). Resigned from office after the scandal of national budget embezzlement. He died before the announcement of the court verdict in January 2008.

2. **Ferdinand Marcos, the Philippines (1917 - 1989).**
President and dictator of the Philippines between 1965 and 1986, who is thought to have stolen a sum of approx. USD 5-10 billion. Fled to the US after witnessing accusations of corruption, mass protests and military coup. Died in Hawaii, in 1989.

3. **Mobutu Sese Seko (Josef Desire Mobutu), the Democratic Republic of the Congo (1930 - 1997).** *Stole approximately USD 5 billion. The country suffered great poverty during his rule. Overthrown during the civil war, fled to Morocco (died of cancer).*

4. **Sani Abacha, Nigeria (1943 - 1998).** *Stole approx. USD 2-5 billion while in office. Became president during the coup that took place in 1993. The dictator died in his own bed with two prostitutes in 1998 from an overdose of Viagra.*

5. **Slobodan Miloshevich, former Yugoslavia (1941 - 2006).** *Looted around USD 1 billion while in office. President of Serbia starting 1989, and later also the president of former Yugoslavia - until 2000. Accused of corruption. Died in the Hague International Tribunal prison in 2006.*

6. **Jean-Claude Duvalier, Haiti (1951-2014)** *Stole USD 300-800 billion. Ruled Haiti from 1971 to 1986. Fled abroad after a military coup.*

7. **Alberto Fujimori, Peru (1938 - 2000).** *President of Peru who looted USD 600 billion during his time in office. He had two terms as president. Resigned in 2006 and fled to Chile, but has been returned to Peru and sentenced to 6 years in prison for embezzlement of public funds.*

8. **Pavlo Lazarenko, Ukraine (born in 1953).** *Stole approx. USD 110-200 billion. Was the Prime Minister of Ukraine between 1996 and 1997. Was suspended by presidential decree after his corrupt connections surfaced. Arrested in the USA in 1999 and sentenced to 9 years in prison.*

9. **Arnoldo Alemán, Nicaragua (1946 - 2002).** *Stole USD 100 billion, served as vice president of the state between 1972 and 2002. Accused of embezzlement of public*

funds and financial laundering through foreign banks. Sentenced to 20 years in prison.

10. **Joseph Estrada, the Philippines (born in 1937).** *Stole USD 70-80 billion, served as vice president of the state between 1992 and 1998 and president from 1998 to 2001. Overthrown through peaceful revolution. Received a life sentence.*

The United Nations and the World Bank have urged the nations of the world to unite their efforts against corruption and the prevention of transferring stolen money to foreign countries. Countries that have suffered presidential corruption tend to have a really hard time recovering funds that have been transferred to foreign banks and cleverly hidden in the process. It took 18 years for the Philippines to recover the USD 624 billion that former President Marcos had stolen. Only half a million dollars of the total looted by Sani Abacha up to 1998 have been returned to the state in 2006. It is thought that the millions of dollars embezzled in post-Soviet states during the first years after the fall of the Soviet Union will never be recovered. Many facts have also surfaced concerning the billion-dollar wealth of uncertain origins owned by people like the President of Iraq Saddam Hussein, President of Libya Muammar Gaddafi, President of Egypt Muhammad Hosni Mubarak, President of Ukraine Viktor Yanukovych and quite a few presidents of other states.

As the saying goes, “man does not live by bread alone”. This is also backed by the fact that not everyone who has money is happy. For example, although Singapore is the 5th country in the world by GDP per capita (~USD 55 182 per person), according to Gallup polls, Singapore’s citizens are the least happy people in the world out of 148 countries. So, advice on taking Singapore as an example of presidential state governance should be viewed with caution lest we want to make the people of our country even more unhappy.

It should be kept in mind that Europe does not have any presidential republics aside from the Eastern countries (France is fundamentally a half-presidential republic). When it comes to South America, however, there is no other place in the world where presidential systems are more popular, and then again – there is no other place in the world that has more coups and revolutions. For example, in the 1970s Argentina had 10 presidents both legitimate and non-legitimate, and in the first decade of this century it has already had 7.

Argentine presidents in the periods 1966-1981 and 1999-2012[37]

1966–1970	**Juan Onganía**
1970–1971	**Roberto Levingston** (not elected)
1971–1973	**Alejandro Lanusse** (not elected)
1973	**Héctor José Cámpora**
1973	**Raúl Alberto Lastiri**
1973–1974	**Juan Domingo Perón**
1974–1976	**Isabel Martínez de Perón**
1976	**Military junta** (not elected)
1976–1981	**Jorge Videla** (not elected)
1999–2001	**Fernando de la Rúa**
2001	**Ramon Puerta**
2001–2002	**Adolfo Rodríguez Saá**
2002	**Eduardo Camaño**
2002–2003	**Eduardo Duhalde**
2003–2007	**Néstor Kirchner**
2007–2012	**Cristina Fernández de Kirchner**

37 Argentina. - www.wikipedia.org

So we can make our own judgments about whether a country with such frequent changes in government as Argentina can have a normal life and a strong state.

Some people who are dissatisfied with the government of their country think that it should be saved, if only a strong hand were to take the wheel of the state, and so they suggest adopting the presidential system. Generally, entrusting all the responsibilities of the state to one person, especially in a country where there is no established tradition of a strong civil society, is a dangerous matter. Life quality research in various countries shows that people are happier, the state is more prosperous and government expenditure is smaller in countries where the parliamentary system is adopted and the parliament is made up of two houses.[38]

Life experience shows us that both extremes have the same number of flaws. The same, according to Sartori, can be said both about sheer presidentialism and parliamentarism,[39] so the only solution seems to be a semi-presidential republic. In such a system, the president is elected through a general election with the requirement of an absolute majority. He then promulgates and announces the bills that parliament passes, while still retaining a right to return these bills to the parliament for reconsideration.

Sartori suggests granting parliament the right to assign a cabinet only once or twice during the whole term in order to protect the government from frequent changes in administration. If this causes yet another collapse of the government, the state should move on to a presidential

38 J.E. Lane, Constitutions, chapter 9.

39 G. Sartori, Comparative Constitutional Engineering, chapter 7.4.

system. In a situation like this, the president should be allowed to appoint and dismiss ministers without the approval of the parliament, but should not be allowed to dissolve the parliament itself.[40]

40 G. Sartori, Comparative Constitutional Engineering, chapter 7.4.

A Minimal Cabinet with a Minimal Apparatus

Cyril Northcote Parkinson's law,[41] which was announced in the middle of the last century and was later confirmed by mathematicians, shows that government agencies have a tendency to expand, finding new horizons for their activities and thus justifying their needs for increased staff. Having analyzed UK governmental institutions, Parkinson also noticed that the number of officials had grown 5-7 percent per year, despite the fact that neither their area of work nor the amount had grown (if there was any work to begin with). These tendencies can be observed in other countries as well. Canadian bureaucracy grew significantly in the last century, when the vast and growing number of government departments and their staff started to seriously hamper the growth of the state and the well-being of citizens. Expenditure of the bureaucratic apparatus had reached 67 percent of the country's GDP. So the system was reformed in 1993 and 1997. This radically decreased the number of government agencies. 9 out of 32 ministries were eliminated and 350 000 people (every sixth civil servant) were left jobless. And most importantly – the state did not collapse and the state government or the lives of the people did not worsen because of the reform. It is natural for countries to have fewer ministries. Switzerland makes do with 8, Japan fares well with 12, France – with 13, and in 1989 the USA had only 14 ministries.

---

41 N.C. Parkinson, Parkinson's law or the Pursuit of Progress.

When taking up the task of government reform, knowing the experience of France might prove useful. In pre-war France, the first governmental Administration Institute in the world was established, and it received a lot of praise in the field of state government organization. When Léon Blum became the Prime Minister in 1936, a state reorganization project[42] was prepared with the help of the same institute, and it was geared towards having six ministries: 1) Ministry of Internal and Legal Affairs; 2) Ministry of External Affairs and Defense; 3) Ministry of Economics and Work; 4) Ministry of Culture and Social Affairs; 5) Ministry of Finance; 6) Ministry of Public Works and Construction.[43] The law of government reorganization of the state of France was passed in July 12 of 1940, but was terminated by the war and the subsequent occupation.[44] The war demanded the establishment of ministries for war victims and veterans, as well as construction and public works, and the other ministries remained separate.

Until now government practice has been as follows: when an agency, department or any government organization is established, the number of its internal departments is determined, as well as its offices and its leader, who must then prepare the policies of the agency within a certain time. The new leader of the organization prepares these policies so as to allow him to be a popular leader with a considerably easy workload and minimal responsibilities, when in fact the sequence in any field of work as well as the field of government work should be entirely the opposite. First of all, the mission of the organization should be chosen, in other words – its purpose,

42 L. Blum, La reforme gouvernementable.

43 "Komba", 1963-01-25.

44 Krylova, I. Apparat gosudarstvenogo upravlenija sovremennoi Franciyi.

and then the goals and desired results should be determined as well.

An effective governmental system should also be one that functions in accordance with the duties, rights and responsibilities principle that we have discussed in Chapter 1. It is only with these prerequisites in action that can we define the subordination and communication connections between the departments and form the organizational structure of the agency administration. After this, the policies of the agency can be formed. And it is only once this sequence of events has been followed that the agency leader should be appointed.

Considering all these principles, a state reform should be started at establishing mission statements for all government agencies. And only then can their structure be addressed, although it has been customary to use the opposite structure in the past.

When preparing a state reform project, it would be smart to consider the progress of humankind and society. The progress of society is determined by the creation of something new, and then that discovery in turn finds its way into life. Usually it begins with art. A new work of art makes humankind change its point of view and look at the world differently – it gives rise to new associations, thoughts of things being not what they have been thought to be. This set of new associations encourages new hypotheses, and when they have analyzed these, people make new discoveries, form theories and test the ways these theories influence life. This is the domain of science. By using discoveries and theories, inventions are created. This is the art of technology. The fact that a caveman tied a rock to a stick and made his first tool which enabled him to kill an animal that was bigger than him more easily was the newest discovery of art, science and technology at the time. And although not all innovations find their way into the world through a sequence like this, the ones that do not should be viewed as mere exceptions. That is why it is first and foremost art and science that creates new ideas and gives impulses to new surges of growth.

In order for works of art or science not to be put in a drawer for safe keeping, but instead enabled to become a valuable asset of public property, they should be broadcast into human minds through education, media, museums and theatres – in order to raise the level of culture in society. This is work that belongs in the field of culture in the broad sense, and which determines the progress of the governmental system as well as the improvement of people's lives. Research into the lives of many states has shown that those countries, which have experienced strong growth in prosperity and citizen well-being, have deemed culture in the broad sense (or more specifically – education) as the agent that determined this change.

That is why in order to ensure the growth of a state, a **Ministry of Culture** which would unite the potential of art, science, education and other fields of culture is necessary first of all. This means that its mission would be to engage in activities that allow society to be highly cultured and ensure the conditions for all members of society to be able to improve themselves in terms of the culture all their lives, starting from their youth.

One of the most important factors that determine the happiness of an individual is his health. Considering this, state reform should start with the system that ensures the health of the members of society and its mission should be to conserve the health and the ability to work of every individual, and those who cannot take care of themselves anymore should be duly supported by the state. This is determined by clean air and a clean environment, a rational way of living, good nutrition, disease prevention and treatment as well as social support. This mission should be carried out by the **Ministry of Health**, which should unite the fields of environment protection, health care and social care services. The Ministry of Health would direct matters of state politics concerning environmental protection (including nuclear safety), as well as the protection and usage of natural resources (land, forestry, water and fossil fuel), it would deal with the fields of geodesy and the care of natural monuments, sanitary services, hygiene and healthy lifestyle education, sports, health care and drug control, health insurance, social insurance (old age pensions), social support and work safety matters. Considering that the function of forests is to serve as "the lungs of nature" (the lumber industry should be a secondary consideration), the forests should fall within the domain of the Ministry of Health.

Having formulated another mission - ensuring that every individual has the resources needed for living (food, clothing and shelter), we can see that another institution is necessary: one which would ensure the conditions needed to form the production and service realization politics of all forms of industry and property (private, group, municipal or governmental) and would also improve the legal conditions of citizen employment and conditions for companies. The **Ministry of Economy** could serve as such an agency, and it would have to unite the matters of production and service industry, agricultural industry, working industry (supply of labor, labor relations, national labor exchange), construction industry, manufacturing industry and commercial trade. This department should control the activities of all fields of business.

Similar reasoning would lead us to the conclusion that a state industry can thrive rationally and purposefully only provided that it has a well-developed infrastructure. That is why a **Ministry of Infrastructure** is needed, its mission being to supply the needs of industry and society in terms of energetics, transportation and all sorts of communications.

A country also needs a **Ministry of Internal Affairs** to ensure the universal safety of citizens and the maintenance of public order in the state.

It may be too audacious to say this today, but we still must consider the fact that in order for citizens to live peacefully and engage in creativity, the international environment must also be conducive to it, and that is why the primary concern of the government should be to ensure the safety and integrity of the country, as well as the peaceful coexistence with neighboring states and other countries through diplomacy - which is a mission for **The Ministry of Foreign Politics**, one that would unite the current departments of Foreign Affairs and State Defense. The potential of both the ministries of foreign affairs and state defense that are traditional in most countries can be united - especially because both of those ministries usually have departments that overlap. Every country normally has general staff which takes care of the matters of state defense as well.

It is understandable that in order for all these ministries to be able to function well, they need to be supplied with financial resources, which should be the mission of the **Ministry of Finance**.

No government system can function reliably without effective feedback. The offices that should ensure this feedback in our case should be the **Statistics Department** and **The Government Accountability Office**, which would come under the government or perhaps the parliament.

And now we can see that we have covered all the fundamental spheres of life of the people and the state with only 7 ministries. This number of ministries allows a government to function properly. Of course, every country still needs safeguards against the establishment of new institutions and the increase in civil service staff.

On the other hand, we cannot wait for good order to establish itself when government work is being done by incompetent individuals, who do not know even the elementary principles of effective administration. That is why the education and constant in-service training of all levels of staff is one of the main contributors to the prosperity of the state and the well-being of its citizens.

Municipality Reform

Nowadays citizens of most countries do not feel that they play any role in the matters of state or municipal government, and so a certain level of apathy arises during elections for offices that should represent their interests, as well as the improvement and control of civil service work. This makes the task of beating corruption and bureaucracy harder, as well as putting a stop to the procrastination of important decision-making in government departments. Municipal reform could and should be implemented in order to encourage citizens to have a stronger public spirit, to remove their despair and encourage their trust in themselves, and inspire them to take action to deal with their own affairs.

The endless talk of municipal reform and direct mayoral or elder elections shows that it is high time for municipality reform. But the mayors who do not want to give up their dominant positions keep the issue from being resolved. The current municipal systems of most countries do not allow citizen participation in the decision-making process of the municipal system, and the municipal accountability mechanism is not effective. Most regional and city governments make their own decisions and are not controlled by the citizens, and central government control is also not effective. Some of the EU municipalities do not conform to the provisions of the European Charter of Municipal Liberties, they still have a single-stage local municipal system, which does not oblige the local government to adequately cooperate with citizens and represent them at the local political government level.

As we have mentioned before, one of the biggest diseases of a government – the general lack of responsibility – is especially relevant at the municipal level. The local government is effective when the mayor is honest and cares about the interests of the people more than he cares about his own. Unfortunately, that is not the case everywhere. That is why when considering municipal reforms, government reforms or any other reforms, we must think of how they will affect the personal accountability of officials. Even the current municipal system has cases of mayors hiding their dirty tricks under the guise of collegial council decisions and then they are not held accountable for the consequences even in the case of clear damage to the citizens or the state. Saying that collegial responsibility is no responsibility at all is not just a metaphor.

The matter of direct mayoral elections is often raised in countries where they are elected by the local council. However, we should consider the fact that if we allow direct elections without changing the system of municipal government itself, we might make matters even worse and “breed” even more scheming supporters, fantastic exploiters or other types of con artists who would rule the city as kings without even a shadow of responsibility for their dark deeds.

Municipal reform through the introduction of direct mayoral elections would indeed have a purpose if it would guarantee the mayor higher powers as well as higher responsibility. This could be achieved by complying with the principles of separation of powers and the correlation of duties, rights and responsibilities.

In our opinion, a directly elected mayor should be the one to divide credit and have the right to suggest his own budget and resolution drafts to the city council. Apart from the mayor, a group made up of no fewer than 7 council members should be able to present resolution drafts as well. These 7 members should be able to function as a sort of safeguard against minor, locally oriented and completely unnecessary drafts. The resolutions approved by the council and signed by the mayor would then be put into action by municipality departments. If the mayor were to see that it would be impossible to adopt the resolution under the local conditions, he should be able to return it for a review based on his motivated reasoning. The mayor would still have to sign the resolution if three quarters of the council voted in favor of it during the review, however, he would not have to carry any material responsibility for the consequences of enacting such a resolution, whereas the council members that have lead him to sign it would not be able to avoid liability.

Responsibility for the consequences of a resolution that have been legally proven to cause harm to citizens or the state should be borne materially by the mayor and all the council members equally, except for those who voted against the resolution in question. Those who have not taken part in the vote or have abstained, should not be held liable, provided they have presented a protest against the resolution in written form within a week. A similar practice is used to ensure the responsibilities of corporate shareholders. Responsibility of municipal council members for collegial decisions that have had consequences harmful to citizens or the state is enforced in the municipal law of some countries, for example, the Danish municipal law (art. 86).

Municipal centralization is different throughout the countries of the European Union. In Lithuania, a municipality has 66 000 citizens on average, in Estonia it has 4 700, in Latvia – 3 000, in the Czech Republic – 1 700, and in France – 1 300.

There are countries where neighborhood offices have been reduced to entities formally dependent on the municipality that have no real rights, and the prefects serve merely as the mayor's subjects and are more inclined to please the mayor than to busy themselves with working in the interest of their citizens. In such countries, regional departments have little influence on the establishment or termination, renovation and otherwise taking care of the important business in the departments of education, health care or culture even if they are based in their own region. In these cases, the opinion of a prefect matters little to the municipal bureaucrats.

When considering municipal reform, the Swiss practice should be taken into consideration. All the questions that can be solved by the community without the aid of higher institutions are settled by the Swiss municipality (Gemeinde) itself. The municipalities build and renovate their own schools, hire teachers and confirm the school curriculum. The federal government decides the general educational politics. The Swiss municipalities provide social care for those in need, are responsible for women's help centers and orphan care homes, manage public order and public transportation systems, build recreational spaces and organize recreational activity programs to a certain level from their own budgets. The water supply and sanitation systems, fire brigades, waste collection services and all other facilities of daily consequence are also the responsibility of municipalities. Usually, a local parliament is elected, and the municipal administration is always at work, although traditionally many questions are still settled in citizen assemblies and through referendums.

The local governments of Switzerland have their own budgets which are made up of tax defined by the federal parliament. However, depending on the community needs, the office can manipulate the size of some taxes to a certain degree. The local government regularly accounts for the usage of funds to the citizens. Nobody can deny that the size of the budget influences municipal services, but the general opinion is that the budget is not the deciding factor when it comes to the efficiency and the quality of services. The level and development of social culture mainly depends on the attitude to human resources, their motivation, the quality of services and only then the budget.

Every country which is going through a municipal reform should ensure that the local government becomes an integral part of the democratic state government, and that through the cooperation of the municipality and the community, an environment would be created in which citizens, apart from certain exceptions, would be able to solve all of their social, property, financial, domestic, cultural, legal and many other problems without having to leave the region of their municipality. The enforcement of this principle would reduce the distance between man and government, and the lower levels of it would start working in the interests of the citizens not only formally, but factually as well. The hierarchical pyramid of control would be flipped upside down.

Having enforced the said reform, the local government would have its own independent budget, which would depend on the number of its citizens, the size of its territory and the character of the region. This would allow it to perform its own organizational, industrial, financial, cultural and ecological activities. The local government should receive full possession of all the premises and any other property that is in the region and which used to formerly belong to the municipality. All of the overland routes should also be handed over to the local government.

Considering the general conclusion that educational development matters can not be settled purely through financial calculations, as was often the case at the beginning of the century, the local government should be given the right to make independent decisions on the opening and closing of schools and their development along with the community. If the question of closing down a school due to budget constraints were to come up, the local government should have the right of organizing fundraising events to aid parents to collect the extra funds required.

The local government should have the right to independently establish social care centers, give financial or any other type of aid to cooperatives and other companies in their own region, to issue permits for the establishment of production units based on individual or group property as well as individual artisans. It should be able to foster, support, develop and control the businesses in its region. The local government would be more interested in doing this if a certain part of the tax were to go to its budget.

The activities of the local government would have to be reviewed no less than once a month by the local council.

The community elder (headman) should be elected directly. The local council should not have any permanent employees. Instead, it should be served by the elder's staff, and the local council chairman should change every six months in alphabetical order of the surname

The elder would perform the functions of the executive government, similar to a certain degree to the functions of a mayor. He should have the right to introduce resolutions and budget drafts to the local council. He should also have the right to veto a decision when, in his opinion, the council resolution is impossible to implement. In this case, he should have the right to ask for a council review, by explaining why exactly it is impossible to implement. If three quarters of the council members are still in agreement on the resolution, the elder should have to implement it, but he would not have to bear the material responsibility for any harm done to the citizens or the state because of the resolution in question. The council members who voted against the resolution and have handed in a written protest within a week would also not bear any responsibility.

Enforcing the suggested municipal reform would diminish the distance between the government and the citizens and the principles of subsidiarity and democracy would be retained.

How Can Corruption Be Beaten?

Despite the fact that many countries have declared war on corruption and developed many programs and implemented many measures to fight it, corruption has not yet been beaten. Corruption is the malevolent exploitation of official powers in one's own selfish interests. Selfishness is inherent to everyone – it is a natural trait that shows an individual's sense of protecting his well-being which he might direct towards himself, towards his family and offspring, or a certain group of people that he belongs to. It's a quality that encourages the development of humankind. However, in the cases of selfishness directed towards illegitimate ends, overshadowed by dishonesty and lack of sense of duty when a person does not understand the responsibility he must take for his own acts, selfishness breeds corruption.

The most common forms of corruption are bribery, abuse of office, influence peddling, protectionism, nepotism, tax evasion, fraud and cartel agreements. Corruption analysis shows that the most conspicuous instances of corruption (the so-called "petty corruption"), for example, bribing police officers, healthcare workers, university teachers – is not the most harmful kind of corruption. One that causes more harm is called "grand corruption", and it occurs in higher spheres – legislation, court verdicts, privatization dealings, public procurements, and concession negotiations. This is the kind of corruption that distorts the economy in an extreme way, causes political lawlessness, encourages business dealings at the informal level of the economy (the grey economy sector), leads to less tax revenue and slows down the economic growth of the state, making it less attractive for investors.[45] It breeds inefficiency and dishonesty in the division of state profits and funds.

Defeating widespread corruption in office is one of the most complicated tasks of any government. It is customary to think that corruption cannot be completely stopped; however, certain measures can be taken to reduce its extent and mitigate its effects. We must agree with the opinion of corruption researchers that using punitive measures alone will not be sufficient and other ways of fighting it must be found. Having ascertained that the usual methods will not help beat corruption, endeavors should be made to find new ways and measures. One of the first things that should be done is to eliminate conditions that are particularly conducive to corrupt practices. If the suggestions presented in this book were to be put into action, the conditions for political corruption to thrive would be less favorable and more restricting.

The measures that could and should be used to reduce corruption:

1. Considering that it is mostly the right of granting privileges or imposing penalties that tempts most officials into corrupt practices, certain norms must be put in place, so that officials have limits on the rights which they have and they cannot change these limits themselves. For example, instead of defining a fine of "1000 to 10 million dollars" for smuggling, a clear guideline of "a fine that is 100 times greater than the value of the goods" should be defined.

---

45 S. Rose-Ackerman, Corruption and Government: Causes, Consequences and Reform, chapter 2.2

2. Government offices should be required to publish all public procurement procedures or calculating and dividing funds (for example, for old age pensions, benefits, privileges), so that any member of the public would be able to access this material freely and be able to notify higher authorities of possible violations without difficulty.

3. In order to put a stop to the use of building permits or other legal documents being obtained through corrupt practices, it must be defined that any permit or other legal document issued contrary to the law would be considered invalid right from the moment of issue. Considering that ignorance of the law is not an excuse, all the expenses incurred through the use of illegally obtained permits should be covered by whoever obtained it, and not the government. This would motivate those requesting the documents to ensure that officials adhere to legal practices and do not break the law.

4. As in the Taiwanese practice, the person who has bribed an official should not be considered a criminal,[46] if he were able to prove or helped prove that the bribe was accepted, even if he had not notified the authorities about the bribe previously. Of course, this method is destructive in legal terms, but it would prevent the briber from hiding the transaction, and in turn it would make the exposure of the corrupt official much smoother. In a way, this would function as the "Sword of Damocles", figuratively speaking.

5. In regard to legal institutions, companies participating in public procurement processes or otherwise providing services to the government should not be granted the right to have trade secrets.

6. Informers who have helped start or win corruption cases should be awarded 25-30 percent of the amount recovered in trial.

---

46 S. Rose-Ackerman, Corruption and Government, chapter 4.5.

7. Citizens should be granted the right to defend violations of public interests in court.

8. A universally practiced declaration of income and assets should be introduced. The declaration procedure should be simple – by filling out a form, the proprietor should be able to evaluate his property based on the market price, and no additional papers would be required. Declaration data should be freely accessible to the public.

9. It should be defined in the law that the only property legally not allowed to be violated is property that has been procured and used through legitimate means.

10. All the processes of public procurement should be transparent, and the failure to ensure this transparency should be viewed as a crude violation itself.

11. A special direct phone line for citizen complaints should be established. It should guarantee complete anonymity and ensure that callers would have no fear of reprisals.

If all these and perhaps some other measures were to be put into action, most citizens would be able to ensure the smooth running of their business in governmental and municipal departments and the influence of corruption could be expected to diminish significantly.

The Death Penalty Issue

Capital punishment as a form of penalty has pros and cons just like any other matter - any thing, any phenomenon, any method or measure. There neither can be nor is there any thing in this world that would be either absolutely positive or absolutely negative. On the other hand, the death penalty is often studied quite one-sidedly: only through the legal and moral attitude, in other words - through its value. It is not exceptional to consider it through the economic, psychological and other attitudes. Each of these attitudes is quite limiting and cannot be trusted separately from the others, and that is why a complex systemic attitude must be considered.

Alvin Toffler has shown that in the old days, government used to use force (violence) in order to make people do what it wanted them to do. In time, the role of violence diminished and power through wealth (money) started to dominate. Later on, knowledge became the main source of power. Although there are many ways to use leverage in authority, the most important ones are force, wealth and knowledge (in the broadest sense). This is what most other resources of authority depend on. According to Toffler, today knowledge is an indisputable source of power of the highest quality.[47]

Despite the fact that the roles of these three factors are ever changing, no state can function without their aid. Force,

47 A. Toffler, Powershift: Knowledge, Wealth and Violence at the Edge of the 21st Century, Chapter 2

as well as coercion, is necessary to protect society from criminal acts, to ensure the safety, rights and freedoms of every individual when other means of protecting these are not attainable.

Back in the old days, violence and death penalties were the methods most used by tribal chiefs and later on by the leaders of countries in order to secure their position in power. It was only after the French revolution when the ideas of human freedom and rights were announced, that talk of abolishing capital punishment even began. Some countries decided to stop using this penalty. However, not long after its removal, it would come back again. That is how the death penalty returned and still functions in the courts of the USA in 35 of its states. Russia has revoked and repeatedly adopted the death penalty several times, starting with the 18th century. The last time it was revoked in the USSR was in 1947 and it was adopted again in 1950. Capital punishment in Switzerland for any crime was abolished in 1874, adopted again in 1879, to be abolished again in 1942; it was abolished in 1889 in Italy and adopted again in 1926; in Australia it was revoked in 1920 and returned in 1934; revoked in Denmark in 1930, and returned in 1946. However, most countries stopped using this kind of penalty or abolished it altogether after WWII. At the moment, the death penalty is illegal in all states of the European Union.

At the moment, there are 96 countries in the world that have revoked the death penalty completely, and 9 countries that use capital punishment for certain special and exceptional crimes (for example, war crimes). In 34 countries capital punishment is not prohibited by law, but it has not been practiced for at least 10 years. There are 58 countries, the USA included, that have not abolished this form of punishment neither in law, nor in practice.

Homosexual relations in Saudi Arabia, Iran, Yemen and some territories of Pakistan receive the death penalty.

Regardless of whether the death penalty is used or outlawed in a country, it is frequently applied in the criminal world for its dark deeds as a form of maintaining discipline and punishing members for giving away secrets or failing to perform assigned tasks, as well threatening peaceful citizens against testifying in court or informing the authorities of criminal schemes or planned attacks they have knowledge of.

And when it comes to civilized democratic states, if they wish to reveal crimes, they need to respect human rights and the freedoms of an individual, as well as design many rules and procedures for persecution and administering justice. This means that if the government wishes to reveal a criminal act, it must comply with the rules it set for itself, which must be in accordance with international standards. On the other hand, criminals do not comply with any such rules, and having committed a crime, they still have the right to the general court process accepted in the state. These individuals demand the legitimacy and validity of any accusing information to be proven, they exploit the flaws of witness protection programs and try to threaten the witnesses in order to stop them from testifying in court.

It is common in the criminal world for members of the gang to be killed for having betrayed the interests of their society. Witnesses are frequently threatened and killed as well. The justice system has a hard time dealing with this due to the rules of ensuring humane restraint conditions. For example, the US justice system had a really hard time administering justice to the famous criminal Al Capone (Alphonse Gabriel Capone, 1899–1947) for the killings, racketeering and other crimes he was responsible for, such as illegal gambling, prostitution and bootlegging during the times of the Prohibition, and this was mainly because the witnesses either kept dying the night before the trial, or retracted their statements due to threats. However, being unable to punish him directly, the police came up with a different pretext. They accused him of spending large sums, for example, 1500 dollars per night in a hotel, and gave him a 10-year sentence for tax evasion. He lost his mind during his time in prison, claiming that a ghost of a person he had killed kept haunting him (although no murder was proven).

Organized criminals, as well as terrorists, become more and more daring by exploiting human rights that are universally accepted in democratic states. They unite into organizations and arm themselves with modern resources, threaten the government and public opinion more and more, and the methods of fighting crime become more liberal. It is natural that abolishing the death penalty should be beneficial to the leaders of organized crime, because they have to pay more for contract killings when capital punishment exists, and they are also more threatened themselves than they would be if there were no legal death penalty. Of course, this is also beneficial to the contract killers themselves.

It is commonly thought that furthering the development of democracy in this area would signify a step in the crusade of liberating aggression. Society has to work harder and spend more money in order to guarantee the custody and comfort of criminals not only at will, but also during the time of their sentence. So it should not be unexpected that organized criminals often fund banks out of their accumulated wealth, as well as lobbyist structures and thus have a great influence on the governmental processes of some states.

Also, in the world of organized crime the worst crimes are committed by the "privates" of the criminal world, while the "generals" simply use contract murderers and bombers to do their dark deeds, which they generally do under the influence of drugs. Even if "a private" is caught, he is the one to take all the blame, because he knows that if he were to betray his associates, he would be found out by his own men and punished by death no matter where he was (even if in jail). It is also important to note that most current witness protection programs are usually of little effect and people do not trust them, and so they do not testify against criminals, especially when it comes to leaders of organized crime. There are many examples of gang leaders continuing their work even from behind bars, where their existence is much more comfortable than that of their victims, and this is not only in Italy. All of this makes it harder to fight organized crime.

With today's communication technologies, the former isolation of criminals from society becomes ineffective. These days, despite many prohibitions, criminals manage to maintain constant contact with the outside world and even continue with their crimes of wheedling large sums of money from gullible citizens through the hands of their free accomplices.

People who advocate the abolition of the death penalty often appeal to the moral side of the matter, and that is something that organized crime does not care about in the least. It is not in vain that some political scientists claim that a war is being waged between the criminal world and the law enforcement system. This war, just like any other war, can only be won, provided that the citizens and the military are resolved to protect their state and that there is a certain amount of economic and military technology available for the task. Governments tend to fight in humane ways, and the arsenal of the criminal world is much more potent than that. It could be said that the government fights crime with bows and arrows, whereas the criminal world fights back with machine-guns, or maybe even chemical or nuclear weapons. It is not really a rhetorical question of who can win in this war.

Some authors stress that life and the right to life are two different things. Life is biological, and the right to life has a social origin. That is why only society, meaning other people who feel the duty to protect a particular person's life, can guarantee this right. If other people do not have a duty to protect that person's life when he is born, this right cannot be guaranteed. In some places, baby girls were got rid of, as boys are more important. Speaking of birthrights in countries such as those would be pointless. In general, what a birthright means is that the constitution of the state (the law) gives the right to life to every person who has been born. Logically thinking, if this is a right granted by the law, it can be taken by the law too. This is analogous to article 18 of the Constitution of Germany which states that the rights granted a person by the constitution can be lost (verwirkt) in certain cases as well.[48] The death penalty should not be viewed as a means of revenge. It is much more important for it to function as a measure of prevention that preempts killings or many other major and brutal crimes, especially as a measure of prevention of contracted crime, which is often used by gang leaders.

48 **Constitution of the Federal Republic of Germany.**

Article 18. [Forfeiture of basic rights]

Whoever abuses the freedom of expression, in particular the freedom of the press (paragraph (1) of Article 5), the freedom of teaching (paragraph (3) of Article 5), the freedom of assembly (Article 8), the freedom of association (Article 9), the privacy of correspondence, posts and telecommunications (Article 10), the rights of property (Article 14), or the right of asylum (Article 16a) in order to combat the free democratic basic order shall forfeit these basic rights. This forfeiture and its extent shall be declared by the Federal Constitutional Court.

On the other hand, although the official statistics show that there has been a decline in deliberate crimes in the past several years, the number of missing people has grown, and this number might contain quite a few murders as well. Some murder victims have never been found, even though the murderer has been convicted. Did those people make it into the statistical lists? They did not, because they were deemed missing. And in the year when they were found, they still did not make it into the lists, because they were not killed in that year. Suicide statistics have also grown lately, which might imply homicides disguised as suicides.

When I was in exile in Siberia, near the Laptev sea, I read a message in the newspaper Pravda, concerning the experience of an Austrian psychologist named Bruno Bettelheim, a former prisoner of Dachau and Buchenwald,[49] who only survived because he started analyzing the psychology of the prisoners. That was when I started to take an interest in the mindset of former lager inmates. In those areas, Russian workers were generally former criminals who had previously served their 10 to 15 years of sentence, some of them being released earlier. Until 1944, citizens from outside the Arctic Circle would not be called to service, so when they were released, they would not go back to their homeland, but would rather stay in the North. I worked as a mechanic of mobile cinema back then, I rode dog and deer sleds around the place and had the opportunity to talk to at least a few hundred former prisoners. I came to the conclusion that all of them knew the criminal law very well and I did not meet a single one who was determined not to go back to crime in the future. Perhaps that was due to the Soviet circumstances, in which a person could just about or not at all survive by still being an honest man. People were

49 Bettelheim, B. "Individual and Mass Behavior in Extreme Situations", Journal of Abnormal and Social Psychology, 1943, 38; 417–452.

reduced to getting spare money or food to get by through illegal means. The former lager prisoners would simply reflect on what crimes were worth doing and what were not worth doing and in what circumstances, and also that non-profitable crimes were really not worth "getting your hands dirty for". They would also stress the fact that a crime that could "get you a bullet in the head" is never worth it. I came to the conclusion that soviet lagers did not reform people, but rather taught them to do their crimes in a more refined manner, in order to avoid getting caught by the authorities, and that the only thing that would deter them was the thought of "a bullet in the head". Perhaps if research were conducted, it would return definite results.

Older citizens of the former USSR remember that in 1947, when the death penalty was revoked, crime rose significantly, "The Black Cat" gangs[50] started turning up, people used to be afraid to go out at night. And when it was returned in 1950, crime declined again and people regained their sense of safety. In some Muslim states where the law of Sharia is practiced and the death penalty exists, there is even less crime than in some developed countries.

Every person has a self-preservation instinct, one that prompts a person to protect his own life, so when there is a possibility of capital punishment by a criminal gang, of course the member of the gang will perform his assignments, because he knows he is facing a more humane punishment from the government. Gang leaders use this tactic expertly and are untouchable by the law. If the instinct of self-preservation works inside the criminal gang, why is it ignored in other social relationships?

50 "The Black Cats" – gangs of burglars who used to imitate the sounds of stray cats in order to get the sympathy of residents, who would open their doors to let the cats in and the burglars who then enter the apartment and rob it, sometimes killing the residents as well.

Rising terrorism and organized crime, the failure to isolate criminals from society because of current technology – all form new challenges in the fight against crime. Both those who oppose and those who approve of the death penalty back their cases with research, but they never quote the sources of this research and its methodology. There is no other way out of the labyrinth of opposing opinions than simply using your own logical thinking. In order to get at the root of this problem, to hear the different opinions on this matter, an extensive discussion on the returning or retaining of the death penalty as a form of punishment is needed.

A citizen that does not feel safe cannot lead a happy life, and that is precisely why the death penalty should exist, even if it were not to be used at all for long stretches of time. It would still perform the function of the figurative sword of Damocles. It must be noted that some of the people who oppose the abolition of the death penalty claim that if it were to be revoked organized crime could not be beaten due to the reasons stated above. In their opinion, with the existence of the death penalty, given that there is a possibility for the convicted person to be able to retain his life even after the trial, provided that he supplies enough material in order to condemn the person who has pushed him to this crime (usually the leader of the gang), the potential of the criminal world would be greatly diminished.

Our Task

You have read the main chapters of this book. What comes next? What should I do?

First of all, answer this question yourselves: do you want life in the future to be better? If you do not, there is nothing you should be doing about it. You should throw away this book and forget about it.

But if you want life in the future to be better both for you and your children, as well as your grandchildren, if you want the citizens of your country to be happy, share the ideas proposed in this book with your family members, your relatives, neighbors, co-workers, even if you don't completely agree with the ideas, or might even strongly disagree with some of them. The main thing is that the material is discussed. Open and honest discussion always leads to the truth, and the idea being discussed improves, too. Through discussion, an idea leaves the plane of dreams and settles onto the "sinful world", the possibilities and possible impediments for its actualization show up. This creates the conditions needed to avoid mistakes or at least minimize them. Through discussion, we also constantly improve ourselves. On the one hand, by defending an idea you assemble additional knowledge and use your thoughts, contemplations, your efforts in order to prove you are right, on the other hand – by seeing that your opponents are right in certain aspects, you change your idea as well. That is how the idea discussed becomes your own creation in a certain part, it becomes your own thing which is worth fighting for.

During discussions, you should not forget that democracy, if it is attainable at all, is a form of government which can make a person happy. After all, happiness is a subjective feeling of fulfillment in life, which comes to a person when he satisfies his spiritual cognitive, communication, aesthetic and physiological needs, it is the factual or the conceived equivalent of an ideal and the existent reality. Happiness is connected to the matter of goals and the meaning of life. It is doubtful that other forms of government could guarantee people happiness.

When you discuss something with someone whose ideas are contrary to your own, you must remember that changing an attitude that might have taken years upon years to establish itself in the human mind can be a really tough and complicated psychological process for a person. They must admit to themselves that they have been wrong up to this point. So discussions with those of opposing viewpoints should always be subtle and tolerant.

The author doesn't think of himself to be an indisputable authority when it comes to questions of state governance or to consider the implementation of the propositions and recommendations suggested in this book to be compulsory and immediate in the governmental system of a given state. The aim of this book is to raise discussion about the issues presented in it. We obtain the worst results when society accepts the maladies and does not make any endeavors to alleviate the situation. However, when people reflect on the problems and start talking about them, raise discussions or start looking for answers, a better solution or at least a satisfactory one is normally found and life becomes better. That is precisely what the author of the book wishes for his readers.

Glossary

References

- Bénéton, Ph., *Introduction a la politique [Introduction to politics]*, Renault: Presses Universitaires de France, 2006.
- *The Blackwell Encyclopaedia of Political Thought*, David Miller (Ed.), UK: Blackwell Publishers Ltd, 1998.
- Berlin, I., *Four Essays of Liberty*, Oxford: Oxford University Press, 1969.
- Dahl, R.A., *A Preface to Democratic Theory*. Chicago: The University of Chicago Press, 1964.
- Dahrendorf, R., *The Modern Social Conflict*, Berkeley and Los Angeles: University of California Press, 1990.
- Denhardt, R.B., *Theories of Public organization*, Third edition.
- Dunleavy, P., O'Leary, B., *Theories of the State: The Politics of Liberal Democracy*, New York: New Amsterdam Books, 1987.
- Dunn, W.N., *Public Policy Analysis: An Introduction,* 3rd ed., NJj: Prentice Hall, 2004.
- Dworkin, R., *Taking Rights Seriously, Cambridge*, MA: Harvard University Press, 1999.
- Gloor, P.A., Copper S.M., *Coolhunting: Chasing Down the Next Big Thing*, New York: AMAZON, 2007.
- Gray, J., *False Dawn: The Delusions of Global Capitalism*, London: Granta Books, 2002.
- Hayek von, F.A., *Law, Legislation and Liberty*, Vol. 1, Chicago: Chicago University Press, 1973.
- Held, D., *Models of Democracy* (2nd ed.), US: Polity Press, 1996.
- Hobbes, T., *Elements of Law*, London: Cass, 1969.

- Kant I. *Political Writings*, Cambridge: Cambridge University Press, 1970.
- Lane, J.E. *Constitutions and Political Theory*, Manchester and New York: Manchester University Press, 1976.
- Lane, J.E. *The Public Sector: Concepts, Models and Approaches,* London: Thousand Oaks and New Delhi, 1995.
- Lindblom C.E., Woodhouse, E.J., *The Policy-Making Process* (3rd ed.), New Jersey: Prentice Hall, 1993.
- Manent, P., *La raison des Nations: Reflections sur la democratie en Europe [The right of Nations: reflections on democracy in Europe]*, Paris; Gallimard, 2006.
- Moles, A.A., *Sociodynamique de la culture [the social dynamics of culture]*, Mouton Paris: La Haye, 1967.
- Parkinson, N.C., *Parkinson's law or the Pursuit of Progress*, London: John Murray, 1957.
- Parsons, W., *Public policy: on introduction to the theory and practice of policy analysis*, Cheltelham U.K.: Edward Elgar, 1997.
- Pollitt, C., Bouckaert, G., *Public Management Reform: a Comparative Analysis*, Oxford: Oxford University Press, 2000.
- Putnan, R.D., with Leonardi, R. and Nanetti, R.Y., *Making Democracy Work: Civic Traditions in Modern Italy*, New Jersey: Princeton University Press, 1994.
- Rawls, J.A., *Theory of Justice*, Cambridge: Harvard University Press, 1991.
- Rose-Ackerman, S., *Corruption and Government: Causes, Consequences and Reform*, Cambridge: Cambridge University Press, 1999.
- Rousseau, J.J., *The Social Contract and Other Later Political Writings*, Cambridge: Cambridge University Press, 1992.

- Ruwart, M.J., *Healing our World: The other Piece of the Puzzle*, Kalamazoo, Michigan: SunStar Press, 1993.
- Sabine, G.H., *A History of Political Theory* (4th ed), Chicago: Holt, Rinchard and Winston, 1995.
- Sartori, G., *Comparative Constitutional Engineering: An inquiry into Structures, Incentives and Outcomes*, (2nd ed.), Macmillan Press Limited, 1997.
- Schumpeter, J.A., *Capitalism, Socialism and Democracy*, (5th ed.), London and New York: George Allen and Unwin, 1976
- Simon, H.A., *Administrative Behavior: A Study of Decision-Making Processes in Administrative Organizations*, (4th ed.), New York: The Free Press, Simon & Schuster, 1997.
- Stone, D., *Policy Paradox: The Art of Political Decision Making*, New York-London: W.W. Norton & Company, 1997.
- Thom, R., Ritz, A., *Public Management: Innovative Konzepte zur Fürung im öffentliche Sector*, Wiesbaden: Gabler GmbH, 2000.
- Toffler, A., *Powershift: Knowledge,Wealth and Violence at the Edge of the 21st Century*, : Bantam Books, 1991.

www.ingramcontent.com/pod-product-compliance
Ingram Content Group UK Ltd.
Pitfield, Milton Keynes, MK11 3LW, UK
UKHW041936190726
13854UKWH00004B/1621